MICHIGAN SLAVIC TRANSLATIONS

ANTHOLOGY OF CZECH POETRY

INVE
VE
DVC
Sc

VVEN
CEZLA
TVS DVX

AD ME · ET NON

CZECH POETRY

A BILINGUAL ANTHOLOGY VOL. I

Ann Arbor

MICHIGAN SLAVIC PUBLICATIONS

ISBN: 0-930042-34-4
Library of Congress Card Number: 73-171082
Second Printing 1979

The illustrations were reproduced
by Robert Kalmbach,
University of Michigan Photo Service

Design and production by Leonard Zamiska

Published under the auspices of
The Czechoslovak Society of Arts and Sciences in America
by
Michigan Slavic Publications
Department of Slavic Languages and Literatures
University of Michigan

CONTENTS

ix

ILLUSTRATIONS

INTRODUCTION

Nations whose languages are not widely read and studied beyond their confines have bad luck with the reputation and influence of their poetry. Who, among English-speaking readers, knows much about Dutch, Portuguese, or Swedish poetry, except a few specialists? The minor Slavic nations fare even worse. The great novelists, Turgenev, Dostoevsky, Tolstoy, have forced the Russian poets of the nineteenth century, Pushkin and Lermontov, on the consciousness of the West, though as late as 1887 Matthew Arnold could state confidently that the Russians "have had no great poetry." The rich Polish romantic poetry remains almost unknown in the West, and Czech poetry seems universally ignored. The names of John Huss, reformer and martyr, John Amos Comenius, pioneer of education, and Thomas Masaryk are known and honored in the West, but they are hardly read as authors. They wrote in prose as did the two recent writers who have penetrated abroad: Karel Čapek, whose plays, *R. U. R.* and *Insect Play,* fitted into the post-World-War I polemic against technology and collective fanaticism, and Jaroslav Hašek, whose picaresque novel, *The Good Soldier Švejk,* appealed as a new version of the story of the wise fool: the do-nothing passive resister against the horrors of war and tangles of bureaucracy.

The reasons for the neglect of Czech poetry are not far to seek. No single name has, even in his native land, acquired the luster of a Pushkin or a Mickiewicz. No prestigious translator has devoted himself to Czech poetry, even though attempts were made very early, also in English. John Bowring (1792-1872) published *Cheskian Anthology, being a History of the Poetical Literature of Bohemia with translated Specimens* as early as 1832, and Albert Henry Wratislaw (1822-92), a descendant of a noble Czech family long settled in England, brought out another collection, *Lyra Czecho-slavanská: Bohemian Poems: Ancient and Modern* in 1849. Both these collections, unfortunately, drew largely on the forged manuscripts of Zelená Hora (Grünberg) and Králové Dvůr (Köni-ginhof), which tried to fabricate a mythical past but were actually written early in the nineteenth century. Thus only Paul Selver's *Anthology of Modern Bohemian Poetry* (1912) must be considered the beginning of competent translation of Czech poetry, mainly of the turn of the century. Our collection can draw on Selver's translations, which show his skill in capturing the flavor of Czech verse in similar nineteenth-century English poetic style.

How can one translate Czech poetry—or, for that matter, any poetry—into English? Debates about the proper way have been raging for years. It cannot be settled dogmatically, for the function of a translation and the audience envisaged will differ. One school defends literal, interlinear versions. It has its most renowned advocate in Vladimir Nabokov, who gave us a prose version of Pushkin's *Evgeny Onegin* which is also an elaborate paraphrase and exegesis. Many specimens in our anthology, particularly of medieval texts, use this method, as it seemed more important to convey the exact content than to try to reconstruct remote and ancient styles of poetical expression. The other theory holds, in its extreme, that the translator must produce an English poem without much regard for the original. The translations of Ezra Pound and, more recently, the *Imitations* of Robert Lowell have scored successes, often at the expense not only of what could be called fidelity but often with a deliberate imaginative elaboration and even distortion of the original. Those who know the model will find their favorites often battered and even mutilated beyond recognition. The defense would, however, argue that translations are not for those who know the language, that the translator is or should be a poet in his own right. Most translations in this anthology rather strike a middle road: they try to follow closely the sense of their originals and, at the same time, to preserve a sense of English style and English meter. If, as the Italians say, translations are like women, either ugly and faithful or beautiful and unfaithful, our translators obviously hope that, as in real life, there are some shades in between: pretty faithful and rather handsome. Sometimes the translators fight, admittedly, a losing battle. Czech versification differs from English: the syntax, the diction, the implications of a word or phrase cannot be reproduced exactly. A compromise has to be found which suggests something foreign, something Czech, within the English context.

Somehow the translator must assume (as did Walter Benjamin in his famous essay on "The Task of the Translator") that there is a common poetic language, something like a deep structure which we can reach despite all differences on the linguistic surface. Surely, on occasion, these translations succeed.

But how should we read this anthology? First, no doubt, it offers much of historical interest. It illustrates the history of the nation from the fourteenth century, when Czech replaced Latin (and earlier Church Slavic) to 1918, the date of the establishment of the Czechoslovak Republic. We see the large turning points in history: the flowering of a courtly culture in the fourteenth century, the violent interruption caused by the Hussite wars in the fifteenth century, the Reformation of the sixteenth century, the Counter-reformation of the seventeenth, the slow awakening in the late eighteenth and early nineteenth century, the growth of modern nationalism and a new sense of nationhood in the nineteenth and early twentieth century, when the Czechs at last freed themselves from the long domination by the Holy Roman and later the Austrian Empire, of which they had been a part since Ferdinand I became King of Bohemia in 1523.

Still, poetry is not a mere illustration of social or political history. We might as well read political tracts and documents instead and might learn more. Poetry has its own history, which is clearly, though selectively, displayed in our samples. It is a history of the growth of the language, of the elaboration of a poetic idiom and its changes over the centuries: we can compare the heavily ornate diction of the medieval legend of St. Catherine with the bald pathos of the Hussite battle hymn and contrast this with the elaborately figurative meditations of the Baroque poets of the seventeenth century. We can observe the folksy simplicity of the early nineteenth century and the turn to a fluid and grandiloquent rhetoric at a later stage. We can see Czech poetry paralleling and often mirroring the history of European poetry in its outlines, though its tradition was several times interrupted by the tragic history of the nation. At times, we can discern special local developments. Czech poetry in the fourteenth century was the richest of all Slavic poetries at that time. All the genres of West European literature were represented. Verse romances, rhymed chronicles, verse satires (here represented by *The Groom and the Clerk*), courtly love poems, saints' legends, religious meditations, didactic

xvii

poems, even a versified encyclopedia survive. The versification often shows high technical skill and a handling of language which cannot be explained by Western influence, however strong that was on themes and composition. With the fifteenth century, a decline in poetic skill began which was not remedied even during the sixteenth century. The Czechs had no Renaissance, while in Poland and Dalmatia fine poetry was written. They were then totally absorbed by the religious question; hymns are practically the only verse which, within a didactic setting, preserves some sparks of the poetic spirit. The immeasurable catastrophe of the Battle of the White Mountain (1620) and its aftermath, the Thirty Years' War, paradoxically allowed the flowering of a new poetry. The Czech folk song and ballad was largely composed during these centuries of political isolation. Baroque poetry, mainly written by priests, belongs to the same time. About thirty years ago a group of scholars rediscovered this rich literature, which had been either unknown or neglected because it was Roman Catholic in temper and linguistically belonged to a tradition repudiated by the Czechs in the nineteenth century. It used a diction which was permeated with Latin and German words, a usage which to later times, insistent on pure Czech, sounded barbarous. Besides, Czech Baroque poetry often ran counter to the taste of the nineteenth century, which disapproved of its complex metaphors and its paradoxical feelings about life and death. Our anthology contains several fine samples of this mood. One must admit, however, that this civilization, which was not primarily literary at all, but creative mainly in music, architecture, sculpture, and painting, had its narrow limits. The Czechs lived as if in the stagnant backwater of peasant Catholic Europe. There was not a trace of the intellectual excitement of contemporary England or France.

The Enlightenment and the effects of the French Revolution destroyed the civilization of the Baroque. Literary tradition was again interrupted. Czech again became the language of the educated classes. A new romantic poetry was created which was modelled on the native folk poetry or on the rediscovered epics of the Russians and Serbs. But most of the leaders of the Czech revival were not poets: they were philologists, antiquarians or publicists, propagandists, satirists. Even Ian Kollár was a poet only intermittently: his verse is didactic, erudite, contrived. Only in Karel Hynek Mácha (1810-36) did a great poet arise. The astonishingly close texture of euphony and curiously suggestive diction of his poems can hardly be conveyed in translation. His poem *May* (1836) has a creaky conventional plot which should not, even in translation, obscure the originality of his way of looking at the world, his nihilistic despair, which differs profoundly from the much more comfortable *mal du siècle* of Byron, with whom Mácha has been associated. The later nineteenth century follows then the general European developments. With the advent of Jaroslav Vrchlický (1853-1912), whose enormous output could not be adequately represented in our anthology, Czech poetry broke definitely through its local confines. In rather unfortunate phrases, Vrchlický "opened the windows to Europe." Czech poetry "caught up" with the West, with France and Italy. Vrchlický could write ambitious, brilliant, and, alas, often facile and showy poetry which vied with Victor Hugo, Tennyson, and Carducci. The reaction against him and his imitators was inevitable. It went in two directions: a colloquial poetry concerned with social issues and a symbolist poetry preoccupied with the eternal verities. Petr Bezruč, a Whitmanesque singer protesting against national and social oppression, contrasts sharply with Otokar Březina, whose ecstatic hymns address and embrace all mankind. The great change in poetic style comes, however, only after 1918, with the poets who will be included in the second volume of this anthology. The new volume should show that there is significant and often great poetry in Czech during these last sixty years. It can be compared with any poetry in any of the smaller countries, in scope, subtlety, vivacity, and often profundity.

In the meantime we offer this sampling of six centuries of poetic effort as a historical record of great interest to anybody who cares for the Czech nation and its achievement, but also, independently of any national concern, as a sampling of great artistic wealth. The book should, we hope, accomplish what Goethe said of translators: "they are to be looked at as busy matchmakers who extol a half-veiled beauty as worthy of our love. They excite an irresistible desire for the original."

René Wellek
January 1973

The records of a nation's literature survive as relics of lost ages, when the physical structures raised by men have crumbled away. A poem, memorised, repeated, adapted, and finally committed to writing, fixes for future generations an impression of the society from which it sprang. But the fixing of an orally transmitted composition may be a late development: the first literary records of a people can be conceived not only as a beginning, but also as the end of a long sequence. The record of Czech poetry can be traced back in a more or less unbroken series to the early years of the fourteenth century A.D. Yet behind this again lies a long literary development in which Czech scholarly monks and courtiers composed, not in the vernacular, but in Old Church Slavonic and in Latin. But while "high" literature in the classical languages was the preserve of church and court, prayers and hymns in Czech were composed for use by the commoners on occasions of religious celebration: a few of these have survived, because they became part of subsequent religious tradition. The oldest surviving Czech hymn Hospodine, pomiluj ny, based on a Greek refrain and preserving traces of Old Slavonic forms, is attested in literature from the XIV century; but the first use of the hymn must be much older. It was sung at the coronation of the old Czech kings.

The second hymn here cited, Svatý Václave, addressed to the patron saint of the Czech lands, is dated to the XIIth century. Also the poem, known as Ostrovská piseň, has to be mentioned among the oldest preserved documents of Czech poetry.

1

"Hospodine, pomiluj ny," attested among the Prayers of Jan Milič
from Kroměříž (14th century)

2

HOSPODINE, POMILUJ NY

Hospodine, pomiluj ny!
Jezukriste, pomiluj ny!
Ty, spase všeho mira,
spasiž ny i uslyšiž,
hospodine, hlasy našě!
Daj nám všěm, hospodine,
žizn a mír v zemi!
Krleš! Krleš! Krleš!

LORD HAVE MERCY UPON US

Lord, have mercy upon us
Christ, have mercy upon us
Saviour of all the world
O save us, and lend ears
Lord, unto our prayers.
Grant to us all, O Lord,
Harvest and peace through the land,
Kyrie eleison.

Translated
by Alfred
French

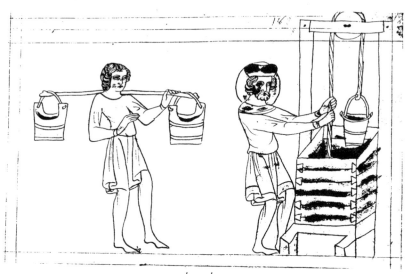

SVATÝ VÁCLAVE

Svatý Václave,
vévodo české země,
kněže náš,
pros za ny boha,
svatého ducha!
Kyrieleison!

Nebeskét' jest dvorstvo krásné,
blaže tomu, ktož tam pójde:
v život věčný,
oheň jasný
svatého ducha!
Kyrieleison!

Pomoci tvé žádámy,
smiluj sě nad námi,
utěš smutné,
otžeň vše zlé,
svatý Václave!
Kyrieleison!

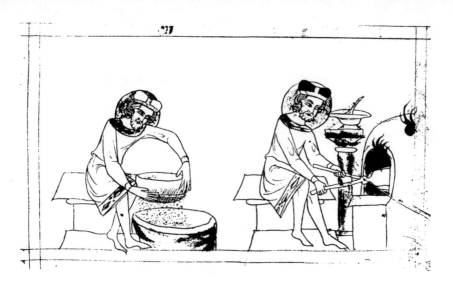

SAINT WENCESLAS

Translated
by Alfred
French

Saint Wenceslas,
Bohemia's noble lord,
our prince!
O pray for us to God
unto the holy ghost,
Kyrie eleison!

Glorious is the realm of heaven,
and blessed he that enters there,
to reach eternal life;
the sacred flame
of the holy ghost,
Kyrie eleison!

On thee we call for aid,
have mercy on us, lord!
raise up the poor in heart,
from all despite deliver us,
Saint Wenceslas,
Kyrie eleison!

Crucifixion from the Psalter of Ostrov (12th-13th century)

6

OSTROVSKÁ PÍSEŇ

SONG OF OSTROV

Slovo do světa stvořenie
v božství schováno,
jež pro Evino zhřěšenie
na svět posláno.

Dievče dřéve porozenie
jest zvěstováno,
z Davidova pokolenie
božsky vzchováno.

Ot něhože náše křščenie
jménem nazváno,
pro drahé náše spasenie
židóm prodáno.

I pro náše vykúpenie
na smrt prodáno,
jehož nám slavné vzkřiešenie
vesele dáno.

The Logos at world's creation
In God's head was kept,
At Eve's sinful transgression
To the world was sent.

To the Virgin the gestation
Is soon announced,
From David's long generation
God's Son descended.

The same holy appellation
For christ'ning was used,
For our eternal salvation
To the Jews was sold.

For the sake of our redemption
He to death was sold,
To us his high resurrection
With joy is given.

Translated
by Mac
Hammond

"Vitaj, králu všemohúci," attested in the Breviary of Lady Kunhuta

he following is an extract from an elaborately constructed hymn celebrating the taking of the Host, and perhaps composed to be sung at the Mass. The work, which is dated to the late 13th century, takes its name from the Lady Kunhuta, daughter of King Otakar II, and Abbess of St. George's Priory in Prague. The style recalls the sophisticated techniques of medieval Latin verse; its mature quality reveals the advance of Czech liturgical writing into the realm of lyric poetry.

KUNHUTINA MODLITBA

Vítaj, kráľu všemohúcí,
ve všěch miestiech vševídúcí,
všěch kajúcích milujúcí,
věčný život dávajúcí;

všeho kvietie kráše ktvúcí,
všěch světlostí viece stvúcí,
svým milým sě zjěvujúcí,
jě rozkošně kochajúcí!

Vítaj, slavný stvořiteľu,
vítaj, milý spasiteľu,
vítaj, věrný náš přieteľu,
všie dobroty davateľu;

10

THE PRAYER OF LADY KUNHUTA

Hail to thee, almighty Sovereign,
Whom we see in every province,
Thou who lovest each confessor,
Thou who givest life eternal:

More resplendent than the flower,
Far more brilliant than the daystar;
Thou who dost reveal thy likeness
Unto all whom thou adorest.

Hail, O glorious Creator,
Hail to thee, beloved Savior,
Hail, O Thou that dost befriend us,
Hail to thee, Giver of goodness.

Translated
by R. G.
Vroon and
A. Levitsky

11

vítaj, v núzi těšitel'u,
všeho hoře zbavitel'u,
vítaj divný slavitel'u
i rozkošný krmitel'u!

Děkujemy tobě z tvého
z milovánie velikého,
z potřebného, z radostného
z vysokého i z ščedrého:

ež si ráčil ny stvořiti,
velmi dražě vykúpiti,
nebesa dens otvořiti
a svým tělem obdařiti.

Chvála tobě, bože, z toho,
ježe činíš divóv mnoho,
divnú mocú slova tvého
v rukú popa všelikého:

tu své divy ty zjěvuješ,
když nás hřiešných navščěvuješ,
chléb v své tělo proměňuješ,
z vína svú krev učiňuješ.

V chlebnéj tváři ty sě skrýváš
božskú světlost tú pokrýváš
cěle v oplatcě přebýváš,
cěle na nebi počíváš;

ani na nebi jsi věcší,
ani v oplatcě jsi menší,
ani na nebi světlejší,
ani v oplatcě temnější.

Na nebi jsi veštek zjěvně,
v oplatcě jsi veštek tajně,
jakož na nebi jsi slavně,
takož v oplatcě jsi divně;

12

In our needs thou dost console us,
In our sorrow dost relieve us;
Thou art worthy of our praises,
Thou dost nurture and sustain us!

And we give thee thanks out of thy
Love for us, a love so plentious,
Necessary and so joyous,
So exalted and abundant:

For in love thou didst create us,
At great price didst thou redeem us,
Opening the heavens for us
Bestowing thy flesh upon us.

Lord our God, we bring thee praises
For the miracles thou makest,
For thy words are full of power
In the hands of priest and father:

Here thou dost reveal thy wonders
When thou visitest the sinful,
Thou dost take the wine and wafer,
Making them thy blood and body.

In the face of bread thou hidest,
All thy godly brightness hidest;
In the host thou art all present,
In the skies thou art all present;

In the skies no greater art thou,
In the host no lesser art thou;
In the skies thou art no lighter,
In the host thou art no darker.

Though we see thee in the heavens,
Thou art unseen in the wafer;
Thou art glorious in the heavens,
Thou art wondrous in the wafer;

13

když tak divně k nám přichodíš,
s sobú anjely přivodíš,
k velikéj čsti nám to hodíš,
když k nám s anjely přichodíš.

Tvé jest tělo naplněno,
divně když jest učiněno,
mocným slovem usvaceno,
věrným srdcem uchvaceno:

to každému jmieti za to,
jež jest srdcem takež vzato,
jakož usty vzemše svato:
Augustin jest svědek na to.

Na to svědka slunce jmámy:
kdyžto na ně vzpomínámy,
mnoho poprskóv vídámy,
avšak jedno slunce známy.

Kdyžto bude rozlomeno,
v malé částky rozdrobeno,
po všem světu rozděleno,
vše křesťanstvo obděleno.

Kakož koli i prokniemu
málo dáno jest věrnému,
avšako cěle jest prvniemu,
cěle dáno i druhému;

cěle dáno jest třetiemu,
cěle také i čtvrtému,
cěle věrně tis'úciemu,
cěle jistě posledniemu.

Avšak proto nenie dvoje
božie tělo ani troje:
ve všěch miestiech vše jedno je,
tako věří srdce moje.

14

Thou dost come with wondrous presence,
Thou dost bring thy angels with thee,
Honoring us with thy presence,
When thou comest with thine angels.

For thy flesh finds consummation
When thy mighty word hath formed it;
It receives sanctification
When the steadfast heart receives it:

Every man should have a part in
Elements the heart has taken,
As one's lips also receive them:
Augustine is witness to it.

And the daystar doth bear witness:
While reflecting on its presence,
We see many rays come from it,
Still we know only one daystar.

If thy body should be broken
Crumbled into tiny pieces
And apportioned to all peoples,
Christendom would be rewarded.

For what little is left over
To be given each believer,
Still the whole is the possession
Of the first and of the second;

All is given to the third one,
All is given to the fourth one,
All is given to the thousands,
All is given to the last one.

For this reason our Lord's body
Being neither twain nor three fold
Shines as one where 'er we find it
And my spirit doth believe it.

15

Dež jest z dievky porozeno,
téže na křížu umořeno,
téže v zemi pohřebeno,
téže z mrtvých jest vzkřiešeno.

Ale tako jest vzkřiešeno,
jakož ovšem oslaveno,
téže na nebe zpodviženo,
téže v oplatcě posvaceno:

ten chléb živý nejde dolóv,
na výsot jde k otcu domóv,
krmě jest všěch apoštolóv
i všěch svatých i anjelóv.

Proto prosím, bože, tebe,
živý i rozkošný chlebe,
aby otvořě dnes nebe
dal nám ščedré dary z sebe.

16

For a virgin did conceive him,
On a cross they crucified him;
In the earth did they entomb Him,
From His grave He rose triumphant.

For thy body resurrected
Is so raised to be in glory
To ascend unto the heavens
In the host to be made holy:

Once transformed, the living wafer
Goes not down but to the father,
As the food of all apostles
Of the spirits and the angels.

Thus I beg thee, Lord our Savior
Live and wondrous in the wafer
Open up the skies this morning
Give us many gifts and blessings.

St. Catherine
(1360)
České Budějovice
South Bohemia

When Czech literature emerges into the full light of day, we find not primitive beginnings, but a highly developed literary situation in which Czech poets and scholars, accustomed to write in the international languages of church and state, to an increasing extent began to compose in their native tongue, bringing it to a cultural maturity which was the product of a long literary tradition. When the ruling dynasty of the Přemyslids came to an end in 1306, Prague was the centre of a powerful Bohemian kingdom which had briefly linked to its dominions the thrones of Hungary and Poland. Under the new house of Luxemburg, in particular during the reign of the emperor Charles IV, Prague acquired a new splendour which established its court as among the most brilliant in medieval Europe.

It was during the reign of Charles IV that the great structures of Gothic Prague were rebuilt in all their magnificence. The rapid economic development of the city coincided with the spread of books and learning, symbolised by the foundation of the Caroline University in 1348. Secular literature now possessed two main centres, in court and university, to maintain the supply of writers and their audience. Among the most interesting achievements of the period is the LEGEND OF ST. CATHERINE, which combines religious, scholastic and secular themes in an accomplished epic poem. According to the legend, Catherine, a royal princess, is converted to Christianity by a pilgrim, and pledges herself to Jesus in mystical bethrothal. Under pressure she remains faithful to Him and rejects the suit of the powerful emperor Maxentius. Sustained by her devotion to her holy lover Catherine remains adamant in face of torture, and as the whips of the torturers cut into her flesh, her body takes on various colours of mystical symbolism—green for love's birth, white for hope, red for love's fire, black for suffering, blue for constancy, and gold for love's ultimate consummation. In physical martyrdom is fulfilled the love of the spirit. The LEGEND OF ST. CATHERINE is only one of a series of Czech verse epics of the fourteenth century. While outstanding in quality it is a typical product of its age, combining as it does the themes of miracles and martyrdom, scholarly disputation and chivalrous devotion.

19

LEGENDA O SVATÉ KATEŘINĚ

Tot' tu dle svého přietele
z šesti barev čistá mesla
u věrnéj milosti nesla,
jakož věrná milá svého
nositi jmá dle milého.
První barvu nesla v spěchu,
ež tě líčci, ješto ktviechu
u biele i v červenosti,
tě sě obě v tej žalosti
změnivše, však krve nezbyvše,
ale krásu svú pokryvše,
zelenásta pravým studem,
ež před tiem pohanským bludem
stáše obnažena jsúci.

A fragment
(lines 2301-
2380)

THE LEGEND OF ST. CATHERINE

Catherine wore from true devotion
marks of love for him she cherished,
stripes of purest hue, six colours,
even as becomes a lover
faithful to the man she loves.
Hot in haste came first that colour
when her cheeks, whose gentle pallor
mingled with the flower of crimson,
now transformed amid her torment
though as yet no blood had left her
masking all their gentle beauty
turned to green, in shame for standing
naked - seen by pagan sinners.

Translated
by Alfred
French

U pravé milosti vrúcí,
spenši svoji rucě k sobě,
zatvořivši oči obě,
hlavu schýlivši sě tiši.
Nad níž ti pohani liší
divoké bitie tvořiechu,
od nichžto ran sě nořiechu
blesky z jejie oči jasnú
v horkých krópkách čilú nečasnú
přes tě líčci dle bolesti.
Druhú barvu bez všiej pesti
nesla dle jiných nádějí.
Ba kteréj jest kdy milejí
byl který chot než té drahé,
ež jejie bělúcie nahé
tělo přěd pohanstvem stkvieše,
na němžto črvená ktvieše
barva ot jejie krve svaté,
kterú ty panošě klaté
zkropichu tu bělost stkvúcí?
Mezi tiem pak mnohú ktvúcí
róži bieše toho časa
znáti z kuože i od masa,
jakž je udicě zahnavše,
mnohé od kosti vydravše
ostavily biechu svrchu:
ty pak zmrtvěvše na vrchu
črnáchu sě bolestívě.
Pátú barvu žalostívě
nesla dle ustavičnosti
svému choti vše k libosti
jako jistá věrná sluha.
Nejedna batožná duha
bolest jí k srdéčku vzdřěhši,
pod koží s krví naběhši,
modráše sě, stezku stáhši,
mezi rány sě rozpřáhši,
kadyž mukař bičem miéřil.

Now she clasped her hands together,
closed her eyes in rapt devotion,
silently she bowed her forehead.
Standing over her the pagans
fiercely applied the lash;
from the blows that rained upon her
sparks were flashing from her eyes,
running in hot tears of anguish
down her cheeks in agony.

Now she bore the second colour,
symbol not of shame but hope.
When was ever wife more loving
than the maid who, standing naked,
dazzling white before the pagans,
wore her pale flesh etched with crimson
from the sacred blood the servants
spread upon her shining whiteness.

In that moment many a rosebud
flowered from the bleeding flesh,
as the hooks that cut within her
left the bones below uncovered
blackened in her deadly torment.

Fifth in order came the colour
signalling fidelity,
which she wore amid her anguish
from devotion to her husband,
as a true and faithful servant.
When the lashes fell upon her,
piercing her heart with pain,
blood that streamed along within her
gathered into angry bruises
where the whip bit in her body;
changing colour into blue.

23

Nesnad bych již tomu věřil,
by nynie která bez omyla
tak věrnéj milosti byla
a svému choti tak přála,
by proň jednéj ráně stála,
ješto svatá Kateřina,
rozkošná dci mateřina,
mnoho set na sobě jměla.
V šestú barvu bieše dospěla,
by sě oděla v též časy,
v něž jejie žádúcie vlasy
tu také trpiechu za to,
jež sě dráže než vše zlato
stkviechu, což ho jest na světě.
Ty sě u zvláštivé přietě
chvějiechu po jejie pleci,
a když ti bičové mecí,
mezi ně sě zapletiechu,
tu je i s pltí vytrhniechu;
pak svězením jdúce za sě
ostaniechu jí u masě,
v němž sě skrzě krev bleskniechu.
Tak sě ty barvy leskniechu
všecko druha přiemo druzě,
zde u masě, onde v duzě,
biele, črně i zeleně,
modřě, žlutě i črveně,
každá v svéj vlastnéj postatě.

24

Hard to credit that a maiden
now exists of such perfection,
so devoted to her husband,
as one blow for him to suffer;
even as Saint Catherine,
lovely daughter of her mother,
bore so many hundred lashes.

Sixth in order came that colour
donned by her upon the moment
when the penalty of beauty
fell upon her lovely tresses
shining in their lustrous splendour
brighter than the gleam of gold.
Quivering upon her shoulders
as the blows beat down upon her,
intertwining with the whiplash
with the skin were torn asunder:
so the hairs remained embedded
gleaming through the blood and sinews.

Thus the colours shone and mingled,
picked out in the flesh and bruises;
white and black and green and blue,
gold and crimson, every colour
faithful to its own true substance.

King David and musicians. Bible of king Václav IV (14th century)

26

With the spread of books and learning the themes of verse epic began increasingly to be written in prose, and epic poetry declined in quality and popularity. But by the end of the fourteenth century Czech literature had developed a fine tradition of lyric verse, influenced by the Provençal love songs and the techniques of the German Minnesingers. The songs are highly stylised and composed strictly in accordance with the conventions of the genre. In one case the name of the writer has survived with his poem: it is Záviš, a Master of the university, whose famous love song contains all the familiar features characteristic of the courtly love poem. Among the most charming of the poems of this time are the songs of dawn—the scene of parting as the rising sun discovers the young lovers still asleep on the grass. Although this poetry is concerned with the traditional themes of romantic love, it can hardly be called personal poetry, because the personality of the writer rarely, if ever, intrudes. The pleasures, passions, and disappointments there portrayed belong to no actual love affair, but rather to the stock-in-trade of traditional romance. The language and the situations are often of a homely nature, so that this highly artificial genre later became easily absorbed into the repertoire of folk art.

27

ZÁVIŠOVA PÍSEŇ

A fragment

Jižt' mne vše radost ostává,
jižt' mé vše útěchy stanú.
Srdce v túžebné krvi plavá:
to vše pro mú milú žádnú.
Svýma zraky skrzě očko
sílnět' střielé v mé srdéčko,
bydlímt' u plamennéj túžě.
Muoj život v túhách nemáhá:
to vše jejie krása drahá
sílnět' mě k tomu připúzie.
Srdce bolí,
sílně ve krvi plavaje
i žádaje,
žádná, tvé milosti, ač sě móže státi.
Ját' nikoli
živ nebudu na dlúzě
v té túzě,
kdyžt' sě zmilitká neráčí smilovati.

* * *

Labut', divný pták, zpievá umieraje,
také já, smutný žák,
umrut' v túhách zpievaje
pro mú milú žádnú, když sě neráčí smilovati nade mnú.
Ach, auvech, má milá,
již si mě umdlila!
Ještě by mě od smrti vykúpila,
by se mnú jedinké slovce promluvila.
Slunéčko stkvúcie,
ruožě světlúcie,
srdce i tělo dávaji v tvoje ručě,
duši mú poručěji bohu milému,
ač mne neráčíš živiti.

28

THE SONG OF ZÁVIŠ

All my gladness now is passing
all my joy is fled for ever;
blood in yearning floods my spirit.
All this for my blessed lover.
Glances past her eyelids flying
pierce my heart and leave it dying,
seared by hunger's passion burning.
Now my life has come to be
void of hope or happiness
pining for her loveliness:
this her beauty does to me.
Anguish sore
floods my weary heart alway:
thus I pray,
Mistress mine, your mercy grant me!
Now no more
can my living soul remain
so in pain
save my love show grace to me.

Translated
by Alfred
French

* * *

Like the swan that sings at dying
sings the dying scholar, sighing
for the mistress high above me
if she will not choose to love me.
Damozel, your eyes destroy
all my heart and every joy:
them from death could yet recover
one kind word unto your lover.
Sunlight shining
rose repining
make my body yours for ever,
unto God my soul deliver,
if you will not choose to love me.

29

DŘĚVO SĚ LISTEM ODIEVÁ

Dřěvo sě listem odievá,
slavíček v keřku zpievá.
Máji, žaluji tobě
a mécě srdce ve mdlobě.
Zvolil sem sobě milú,
ta tře mé srdce pilú.
Pila řěže, ach bolí,
a tvójt' budu, kdet' sem koli.
Srdéčko, divi sě tobě,
jže nechceš dbáci o sobě.
Tvá radost, veselé hyne
pro tu beze jmene.

Ačt' bych já ji zmenoval,
mnohýt' by mě štráfoval
a řka: Proč ty tak slúžíš?
Čemu sě milostí chlubíš?
Neustavičný milovník
jako u cěsty hřěpík:
k čemu sě koli přičiní,
a tomu všemu uškodí.
Ktot' sem, tenž nosímt' pílu,
játt' mám najkrašší milú,
tét' nikomu nepoviem,
sámt' ji s mým srdéčcem viem.

Viera vieřě pomáhá:
kdet' sú dva sobě věrna,
on jí a ona jemu,
nepoviedaj třeciemu.
Mnohýt' sě rád honosí,
ten tajemství pronosí.
Ach, naň! Zlýt' obyčějt' jmá,
nepřějtež mu, ktot' jeho zná.
Poniž on vás tak hanie,
prosímt' vás, panny i panie,
přězdiec jemu ,,ruší nás",
vyscěrčmež jeho pryč od nás!

NOW DONS THE TREE

Now dons the tree her coat of leaves,
aloft now sings the nightingale.
How much I loathe your advent, May!
Swooning, I feel my spirits fail.
I wooed and won a lovely maid:
she drives into my heart a saw.
Deeply the saw's teeth fray my heart:
and I am yours for evermore.
Poor heart of mine, you act so strangely:
to seek no respite from the pain!
Your gladness—all your peace—is dying.
Yet must She be without a name.

And if I should her name reveal
my honour men would fain debase:
"Why must you serve your mistress so?
Why boast you of a lady's grace?"
Like a weed that grows beside the way
is the man who loves inconstantly:
his wantonness will bring him ill;
a universal bane is he.
But I the one that bears the saw;
and Thou the loveliest mistress art.
Our secret I will tell to none,
alone I share it with my heart.

For true and faithful love endures
when each is true to each alone -
true maid to man, true man to maid -
they keep their secret for their own.
But he that speaks in boastfulness
and spreads her secret name abroad,
doth so disclose his wantonness,
and is by all his peers abhorred.
And that he doth yourselves dismay,
I beg you, ladies, fervently
to shun the one that spoils our play,
and drive him from our company.

Translated
by Alfred
French

31

Concordantia Discordantium Canonun. Bratislava (14th century)

32

To medieval scholars, a classic of sacred love poetry was the Wedding Hymn of Solomon, which we know as the Song of Songs: to the Latin lyrics composed in its style a Christian element was imparted by treating the Shulamite's love for Solomon allegorically as the search of the Christian soul for the saving love of Christ. In the following poem, which recalls the Latin verses of Peter Damiani, the unknown Czech poet has set into the familiar material a new element—an echo of the search of Mary Magdalene for the body of the crucified Jesus, and the strange scene of recognition related in the gospel of St. John (20. 11-18).

33

OTEP MYRRHY

OTEP myrrhy mnět' mój milý,
milujet' mě z své všie síly,
a já jeho,
zmilelého,
proňžt' netbám nic na jiného.

Mój milý mně biel, červen, krásen,
jako leteční den jasen.
To div z diva,
žet' sem živa,
proňžt' se mé srdečko znímá.

Vstanúc i pójdu toho dle,
poptám sobě, proňžt' mé srdečko mdlé
řkúc: Batíčku,
zmilelíčku,
zjev mi svú tvář, sokolíčku.

Jehožt' má duše miluje,
viděli ste, zda kde tu je?
Milost silná,
žádost pilná,
k němužt' má mysl nemylna.

Když diech právě o puolnoci,
stržet' mě jeden z jeho moci
tak neznámě
vzezřev na mě
vecet': Přenes mě v svém prámě.

Tehdy já naň vzezřech nice,
domněch se svého panice.
Řiech: Kam koho?
A on: Toho,
jehož ty hledáš přemnoho.

34

A BUNDLE OF MYRRH

As myrrh is my dear love to me,
he loveth me distractedly;
and I love him,
my heart's desire:
his spirit rules my heart entire.

His skin is pale, his color bright;
as radiant he as summer light.
The miracle
my life became,
has set my longing heart aflame.

I will arise and go apart,
to search for him with fainting heart;
and say: 'Dear Lord,
my precious love.
Reveal to me your face, my dove!'

O tell me if ye saw him here,
the one my spirit loveth dear!
My love is firm;
my thoughts abide,
for ever, ever, by his side.

I, wandering at the midnight hour
met one whose face recalled his power:
so strange did he
look down on me:
'Convey me in thy custody!'

I gazed into the face above me,
thinking I glimpsed the eyes that love me.
I said: 'Where? Whom?'
'That one'; said he,
'for whom you search so passionately.'

Translated
by Alfred
French

35

SLOVCE M

Srdce, netuž, nelzět' zbýti,
pravímt' cěle,
anit' sě jest lzě ukryti
již veselé.

Tot' pravím: Za utěšenie
mnět' v světě milejšie nenie
a za tot' mám,
než to mé milé slovce M,
jenž panuje v srdéčku mém
a v tomt' sě znám.

Ač pod nebem jest stvořenie,
nerozomiem,
róže, jiný květ nic nenie,
tot' směle diem.

Tot' pravím: Za utěšenie
mnět' v světě milejšie nenie
a za tot' mám,
než to mé milé slovce M,
jenž panuje v srdéčku mém
a v tomt' sě znám.

THE LETTER M

Grieve not, my heart, there is no cure,
I truly say,
No power can make thee secure
When all is gay.

Translated
by Karel
Brušák

None else on earth shall ever be
Whom I would serve with constancy
In joy and bliss.
Sole my beloved letter M
That can reward and can condemn
My master is.

For creatures all beneath the sun
I do not care,
The rose makes other flowers none
I here declare.

None else on earth shall ever be
Whom I would serve with constancy
In joy and bliss.
Sole my beloved letter M
That can reward and can condemn
My master is.

37

Jestit' jí mílo slúžiti,
ač z milosti,
anat' dá dobrým požiti
vždy v radosti.

Tot' pravím: Za utěšenie
mnět' v světě milejšie nenie
a za tot' mám,
než to mé milé slovce M,
jenž panuje v srdéčku mém
a v tomt' sě znám.

Rač to v svém srdci zavřieti,
než bez smiechu,
ež mně jiné nelzě mieti
za útěchu.

Tot' pravím: Za utěšenie
mnět' v světě milejšie nenie
a za tot' mám,
než to mé milé slovce M,
jenž panuje v srdéčku mém
a v tomt' sě znám.

Tedyt' poviem otevřěně:
V tvét' službě sem!
Anit' změním do skončenie
mé milé M.

Tot' pravím: Za utěšenie
mnět' v světě milejšie nenie,
a za tot' mám,
než to mé milé slovce M,
jenž panuje v srdéčku mém
a v tomt' sě znám.

With zest and delight serve I thee,
For ever wooed,
Who giveth the true in courtesy
The sweetest food.

None else on earth shall ever be
Whom I would serve with constancy
In joy and bliss.
Sole my beloved letter M
That can reward and can condemn
My master is.

Let this be in thy heart enshrined
And gracious be:
No other shall I ever find
To comfort me.

None else on earth shall ever be
Whom I would serve with constancy
In joy and bliss.
Sole my beloved letter M
That can reward and can condemn
My master is.

My life to thee now I commend,
Thy serf I am.
Nor will I change until my end
The dearest M.

None else on earth shall ever be
Whom I would serve with constancy
In joy and bliss.
Sole my beloved letter M
That can reward and can condemn
My master is.

DETRIMENTUM PACIOR

Detrimentum pacior
nynie i v každém času.
Usque ad mortem quacior,
vše pro její krásu.

Regitur nunc racio
vše podlé jejie vuole.
Obnixa turbacio
jakžto meč srdce kuole.

Nam eius absencia
mě smutného pálí.
O felix essencia!
Každý tvú krásu chválí.

Velud solis radius
zrakem srdce projímá.
Eminens ut gladius
túha mě podjímá.

Celi sub cacumine
nelze kraššie tváři,
zodyaco fulmine
rovna slunečné záři.

Electa cordis unica,
nedaj mi zahynúti!
Tua ut sunt punica,
túhút' chci vzplanúti.

Careo hoc famine,
bych mohl vše vypraviti.
Vale in Dei nomine,
ten tě rač uzdraviti.

DETRIMENTUM PATIOR

Detrimentum patior
Without end day and night,
Usque ad mortem quatior
All for her beauty bright.

Translated
by Karel
Brušák

Regitur nunc ratio
In bondage to her word,
Obnixa turbatio
Stabs my heart like a sword.

Nam eius absentia
Tortures me with despair -
O felix essentia
All praise thy beauty fair.

Velut solis radius
Thy eyes have pierced my heart,
Eminens ut gladius
Does cruel desire dart.

Coeli sub cacumine
Fairer than she is none
Zodiaco fulmine
Matching the very sun.

Electa cordis unica
Oh do not let me die!
Tua ut sunt punica
Aflame with love I lie.

Careo hoc famine
To put my plaint to thee,
Vale in Dei nomine -
May He thy Healer be.

41

NOCI MILÁ

Noci milá, pročs tak dlúha!
Po mé milé jest mi túha,
že mi s ní nelzě mluviti.
Komu sě mám utěšiti?

Již mé srdce bydlí v strasti,
v smutku, v túžebné žalosti.
To vše činí nebývanie
u té najmilejší panie.

Milý bože, nedaj dlúzě
po mé milé býti v tuzě! —
Brachku milý, nestyšt' sobě,
nad jinét' chci přieti tobě.

LOVELY NIGHT

You pass so slowly, lovely night!
Forsaken now, I long in vain
to see once more, to speak with her:
no other one could still the pain.

In anguish of desire my heart
is stretched in horrid ecstasy.
No thing on earth may give me ease
unless my mistress be with me.

Dear Lord, I pray, leave me not long
abandoned in my loneliness!
Beloved, pine no more for me!
Above all else I would thee bless.

Translated
by Alfred
French

MILÝ JASNÝ DNI

Milý jasný dni, pročs tak ukvapil,
žes mi mého klevetníčka zbudil?
A den své ustavenie jmá;
tu kdež milých dvé přebývá.
Všemohúci pane bože, milý bože,
rač jich býti obú spuolu strážě!

Od východa slunce větříček věje,
a přěs hory, přěs doly sě chvěje.
Horyt' ječí, lom sě tiší,
ptačstvo křičí, zvěř pospieší,
obádaje, znamenaje,
žet' má noc od nás odstúpiti.

44

RADIANT DAWN

Radiant dawn abruptly breaking,
tell-tale gossip's tongue awakening:
now the light of day discovers
secret meeting place of lovers.
In Thy care, Almighty, take us
gentle Lord, do not forsake us!

From the East a faint breeze carries,
trembling over hills and valleys.
Woodland sounds of night are dying
birds are calling, creatures flying,
scenting in the coming day
how the darkness ebbs away.

Translated
by Alfred
French

Vyšlat' jes krásná, jasná dennicě,
dalekot' mi u plano vyšla.
Tat' mi pospiecháše od hor.
Všeckno stvořenie, lidský sbor
znamenaje vzhuoru vstáti:
čast' sě náma, milá, požehnati!

Jasný sě nám den ukazuje,
nebesat' jsú sě zamodraly,
slunečnát' zářě vychodí:
po němt' mě mé srdce bolí,
po tom najmilejšiem pánu!
Brachku milý, bychva sě my dva spolu objala!

Vyšlat' jest krásná, sličná paní,
užaslat' sě, viděla svítanie,
řekla: Proč sva tak dlúho spala?
Zarmútilot' sě srdce její:
vstaniž vzhóru, choti milý, radosti má,
byt' sě nám žádná hanba nestala.

Najmilejší, poslechni rady mé
a umysliž ty pevně mysli své,
byt' sě nám nezrušila milost
pro toho klevetníka zlost.
Žádnýt' nevie, cot' on mieni,
slušiet' sě nám jeho vystřiehati.

V očit' klevetník s každým dobřě jest,
mát' na svém srdci falešnú lest.
Budiž muž, neb-li žena,
byt' jej každá mrzkost jměla!
Bylt' by každý tovařiš mój,
ukrátilt' by v mém srdci nepokoj.

Ktožt' ruší útěchu milých dvě,
nedajž jemu bóh toho prospěchu!
Po němt' mě mé srdce bolí,
po tom najmilejšiem pánu.
Všemohúcí pane bože, milý bože,
račiž býti obú nají strážě!

46

Now the morning star has vanished,
fading in the distance, banished
past the mountain ranges, warning
of the coming of the morning.
Man and nature stirring tell
of the hour to say farewell.

Daylight pouring down upon us
turns to blue the distant heavens.
Rising sun and spreading light
fill my mind with sudden fright
for the darling of my heart.
Time for us to kiss and part!

Now the lovely maiden waking
sees with shock the day is breaking
calls aloud in sudden fear
"We have slept too long, my dear.
Rise, my dearest lover, hasten,
lest some scandal find us here."

Ponder the advice I offer,
heed the warning of your lover.
Take care lest the love we cherish
by the gossip's malice perish.
None can guess the gossip's mind,
What fresh mischief he may find.

Smiling face and smooth pretention
mask a treacherous intention.
Whether man it be or maiden
be his conscience heavy laden!
Every man my friend would be
who quietens my anxiety.

Prosper not, dear God above us,
him that spoils the joy of lovers,
fills my heart with sudden fright
fearing for my heart's delight.
In Thy care, Almighty, take us
Gentle Lord, do not forsake us!"

47

Smiths and a musician. Krumlov codex (early 15th century)

*C*zech *XIVth century literature produced, beside its courtly lyrics, poems written in more popular vein. Often satiric in note and with overtones of social tension, they refer to the real life of the time rather than to the romantic world of books. THE GROOM AND THE STUDENT is a burlesque in the form of a dialogue between two speakers who vigorously defend their claims and calling. THE BALLAD OF STEMBERG is a lyric-epic, but based on what was apparently a real and recent happening at the time of composition. Written in racy style, it has less in common with the traditional epic than with the folk ballad, with which it is often connected.*

PODKONÍ A ŽÁK

Přihodich se jednú k tomu,
kdež nalezech v jednom domu
právě také v túž hodinu
dva, jenž přišla pohostinu,
ana sedíta na pivě.
Tu učiništa poctívě,
oba právě bez meškánie
dašta mi milé vítanie.
A já, přiblíživ se k nima,
posadich se mezi nima,
jakož často v krčmě bývá,
křičiec: „Paní, nalí piva!"
Jechomt' se v odplatu ctíti,
podávajíc sobě píti.
Poslúchajte tuto právě,
poviemt' vám o jich postavě.

Z těch jeden člověk bieše mladý,
nejmieše známě brady,
na němž sukně šerá, umlená,
a k tomu kukla zelená;
ta také zedrána bieše.
Mošnu na hrdle jmieše,
v niž by vložil, což mu třeba,
mním, že knihy, také chleba;
dešťky jmieše u pasu.
Jakž jej viděch při tom času,
i jinú k tomu přípravú
vše bieše školskú postavú.

50

THE GROOM AND THE STUDENT

Once I happened to be found
In a tavern well-renowned,
As I sat there in the gloom,
Two men came into the room.
They both hastened straight to greet me,
Offered by their side to seat me,
Welcomed me without abuse.
As in taverns is the use,
I sat down between the two,
Greeted them as was their due,
Heard them calling for good cheer,
"Hostess, pour us all some beer!"
We each drank the other's health,
Wishing one another wealth.
Now, good readers, give me ear,
And you'll learn how they appeared.

Translated
by W. E.
Harkins

One of them was but a youth,
Almost beardless still, in truth,
In a doublet gray and worn,
With a hood green and all torn,
From his neck there hung a sack
Where all needful things were packed:
There both books and bread were placed;
tablets dangled at his waist.
He in all his disposition
Seemed a scholar by condition.

51

Druhý, ten se starší zdáše,
vždy sedě bradku súkáše,
na němž kabátec úzký, krátký,
a dosti zedrané šatky;
okasalý tak dvorně,
k tomut' bieše obut v škorně:
tyt' biechu drahně povetšely,
avšak okolo děr cely,
skrze něž viděti nohy.
A také bieše up'al ostrohy,
točenku maje na hlavě.
Tak, jakž jej sezřech právě,
jistět' mi se dvořák zdieše;
hřbelce za pasem jmějieše.

Ten mluvieše, hrdě sedě,
na své špice pyšně hledě,
řka: „Nenie v světě toho,
ani kto má zbožie tak mnoho,
bych chtěl jeho zbožie vzieti
a dvora se odpověděti.
Neb jest tu tolik utěšenie!
V světě ten jeden nenie,
když by dvořenie okusil,
věčně by dvořiti musil.
Ktož mi o lepšiem bydlu praví,
každý se ve lži ostaví.“

Dotud mluvě usta trudi,
až žáka na se vzbudi.
Ten mu k tomu odpovědě
a řka: „Já to dobře vědě
a tomu já také věři,
že páni i také rytieři,
tit' u dvora dobrú mají,
i bohatí, to já znaji.
Ale nebožátka chudí!
Div, že se jim neostudí
pro zlé bydlo jich dvořenie,
neb již věčší psoty nenie.

52

His companion wore a beard
And much older he appeared,
In a coat short, narrow, battered,
Under which his clothes were tattered.
In his dress he seemed a vassal,
A retainer at some castle.
In his leather boots were holes,
And they both had need of soles,
So that I could see his feet
As he sat there in his seat.
On each boot a spur was strapped,
On his head he wore a cap,
At his belt a curry-comb:
All proclaimed him for a groom.

Gazing at his boot tips proudly,
He announced to all quite loudly,
"There is no man anywhere
Whose condition were so fair
I would envy his estate
And my own place thus berate,
For it brings me such fair pleasure,
And of fortune such full measure.
No one who my lot should try
Would exchange it ere he die.
And if any it should scorn,
Faith, his word were then forsworn."

So he spoke and wagged his tongue,
Till the scholar's ire was stung,
And the latter answered so,
Saying, "I indeed do know
And do also stake my faith
That our lords of high estate
Live in comfort in their castles.
But what say you of their vassals?
Those of them who're very poor
Must sharp poverty endure;
Even those who serve in livery
Have their constant share of misery.

53

Tit' se chodiec psotú klonie.
A nad to pak vy, podkonie,
vy ze všech najhorší máte,
kromě že se v tom neznáte.
Byšte se chtěli poznati,
svú psotu popsati dáti,
což vy jie máte, podkonie:
v světě věčšie psoty nenie,
než vy ji trpíte dobrovolně.
Ale naše bydlo školnie,
tot' já tobě pravím hole,
tut' je ve všem pravá zvóle,
i od pitie i od jedenie,
v ničemž nedostatku nenie.
Myt' netrpíme nikdy hladu.
Když již tovařišie sadú,
tut' já dosáhna úkrucha,
nenie partéka tak sucha,
bych jie nerozmočil jíchú,
tiem lekuje svému břichu;
i budemy dobře syti.
K tomu máme dosti píti
pitie ctného do nerody.
Častokrát také vody
napijemy se pro zdravie,
neb jest velmi dobra hlavě.
Ba, od ztravyt' se mámy pyšně,
masa, kúr dosti přielišně —
tot' jest na každé posviecenie,
v ničemž nedostatka nenie:
když to koli u nás bývá,
mámy přieliš dosti piva.
Ale vám miesto sniedanie
dadie políček za ranie.
Však ste jedno za ranie syti,
bývajíce vždycky biti.
Miesto jedenie oběda
kyjevá rána přisedá."

54

For no bondage is so black
As the toil which breaks your back!
And you stablemen accurst
Have of all of them the worst;
But you grooms have not the wit
That your bondage you'll admit,
Or hear to your face described
All that fate's for you prescribed,
For nowhere there's greater ill
Than you suffer of your will.
But a scholar's life is fair;
Never need he ever bear
Any pangs of hunger curst,
Nor need ever suffer thirst.
When we seat ourselves at table,
Then I reach as best I'm able
For a crust of thick black bread,
And the crust with lard I spread,
For no bit of bread's so hard
You can't make it soft with lard.
So we scholars are well sated.
And for us God has created
Many drinks for our fair pleasure;
Water, too, in no small measure
Drink we as we eat our bread;
It has virtue for the head.
We have quite enough to eat,
Nor do we lack fowls or meat
For the feast days of the year,
For which there's no want of cheer,
And at feasts we have, indeed,
Ale and beer more than we need.
But of you the rumour goes
That for breakfast you're served blows:
So you feel as if you've eaten,
When you're always being beaten.
And instead of a fine dinner
Blows fall thick and make you thinner.''

A když žák přesta mluvenie,
dvořák vece: ,,Toho nenie!"
Okřiče se naň hněvivě
a řka: ,,Žáku, mluvíš křivě,
bychom byli hladoviti
u dvora a kyjem biti.
Ach, přehubená partéko,
i co jest tobě řeči této
o nás mluviti třeba,
sám nejsa nikdy syt chleba?
Co dobrého do vás, žáci?
Však ste vy hubení žebráci,
jenž tečete dóm od domu,
hekajíce a chtiece tomu,
by vám dali jíchy mastné.
Auvech, vaše bydlo strastné!
Tut' vám dadie partéku režnú
a s tiem vás pesky vyženú.
Pakli již na vaše ščestie
vám dadie v některém miestě
jíchy nemastné a málo,
vej, kak se vám dobře stalo!
Již se vše zdálo po vóli.
S tiem pak běžíte do školy,
a to s velmi dobrú myslí,
mniec, byšte na hody přišli.
Tut' vás pak starší omýtie,
i chléb i jíchu vám vzchytie
a to všecko zjedie sami.
Jmút' se vás bíti metlami,
budút' se nad vámi mstíti
hněvy, nejsúc dobře syti.
Ach, tot' vám psota nehovie!
Slýchalt' sem dávné příslovie,
žet' žákóm draho vařenie.
Protož ty nechaj svářenie
se mnú, nebt' já také vědě
praviti o vašiej biedě,
což vy jie máte, žáci.

56

When the scholar was quite through,
Then the groom cried, " 'Tis not true!"
Shouted fiercely at the youth,
"Lying rogue, thou speak'st untruth,
Saying we have never eaten,
But are always being beaten!
Why dost thou so falsely boast,
When thyself art like a post.
Why pretend that we want bread,
When thyself art never fed?
Life is bitter for you scholars,
Wretched beggars and vile brawlers,
As you run from door to door,
Groaning all the while the more,
Begging gravy for your fare
Ah, your life is full of care!
Still some crust they might dispense
Ere they bid you hasten thence.
And if luck continue on,
Somewhere you may come upon
Gravy, meatless, with no flavour:
Ah, how luck smiles in your favor!
With the gravy and the bread
All the way to school you tread,
While your spirits are elated,
Fancying your hunger sated.
But your elders are too shrewd:
They seize you and eat your food.
Then they birch you, still displeased,
That their hunger's not appeased.
Poverty is small advantage;
I myself have heard the adage
That a scholar's meals are meager;
Hence, I pray thee, be not eager
To contend with me in strife,
For I know how hard thy life.

57

Ale my, panici dvořáci,
když již za stolem sedem,
inhed na se lúčiemy chlebem.
Myt' nic nešetřímy toho,
neb ho mámy přieliš mnoho.
Tut' nám dadie jiesti dosti.
Pakliže pro jiné hosti
nás kuchaři zapomanú,
inhed já od stola vstanu
i běžím tam sám k kuchyni:
dadiet' mi dosti zvěřiny —
pakli nenie, ale kaše.
Tot' jest vše útěcha naše,
žet' jí ukydá druh druha
a tudy nás mine túha.
Někdy se vladař v mě vpeří
a mě svú holí udeří
v pleci nebo v hlavu ranú.
Inhed já odběhnu v stranu,
tohot' nikakž nenechaji,
od mateřet' mu nalaji;
kromě leč by byla hlucha,
tožt' jiej nepovzní u ucha.
Když pak bude po večeři,
což nás koli dvorské sběři,
béřemy se dolóv s hradu
a netrpiece v ničemž hladu.
Ale vy, žáci nebožátka!
Ach, že vás jest vaše matka
těžce nosivši v životě
přirodila k takéj psotě!
Já se tomu velmi divi,
že ste jedno bitím živi.
Však vás za obyčej tepú,
jednak burcují, jednak svlekú,
vymyšlujíc muky nové,
o vy kaziec metly březové."

58

But we grooms can leave our stable
And sit down at our own table,
Where we, when they give us bread,
Throw it at another's head.
Cries to spare it go unheeded,
For we have more than is needed.
If the cooks forget us brothers,
When they're serving food to others,
Then at once I go a-looking
To the kitchen where they're cooking.
There they serve a goodly feast,
Or if not, then gruel at least.
This we hurl at one another,
Each his fellow seeks to cover;
Thus we make of meals a sport
And ourselves do so comport.
Now and then our steward goes
Past me and we come to blows,
And he strikes me with his staff,
Heeding naught of this I laugh,
Jump aside and curse his name,
And his mother too defame,
So that she may hear a moaning
In her ears like hornets droning.
And if we e'er come too late
For our supper, then we straight
Set off to the town below:
There to sup we often go.
But your life is quite another:
Why did your unhappy mother,
Who had borne you in her womb,
Bear you for so harsh a doom?
For to me it seems surprising
They don't kill you with chastising,
Such their wont is to maltreat you:
Now they shake you, now they beat you,
Every resolutely searching
For new ways to give a birching."

59

To řek, ruku naň opřeže
a žák ho k sobě za vrch doseže,
k tomu jej v hlavu udeři.
Tak se druh v druha vpeři
za vrch tak nelítostívě,
druh druhu hlavu křívě.
K tomu pohlavci suší
pleskají okolo uší.
Tak zaroveň bez rozpači
druh druha pod se tlači;
hrozný hřmet jde o podlahu,
i sen i on búchá hlavú,
nepoddada se druh druhu.
Rvášta se chvíli tak dlúhú,
drúce sobě usta rózno,
až mě by hleděti hrozno.
Nechtě se dívati tomu,
brach se preč z toho domu,
ana se za vrch vláčíta.
Rujtaž se, dokud ráčíta!

Toť jest krčemná příhoda,
neb se pivo pie, a ne voda.
Dnes, ktož rád do krčmy chodí,
častokrát se jemu přihodí,
žet' zvie příhody někaké
a k tomu noviny také.
Mnohémut' se tak zračí,
najviec, ktož se tam omračí,
žet' má doma co praviti.
Avšak se je lépe zbaviti
a v noci, jakž čas jest, spáti,
a doma novin dočakati.

Then the scholar's wrath did flare
And he grabbed him by the hair,
And did strike him on the nose.
So it was they came to blows,
Nor did either seek to spare
His companion's face or hair.
And their battered eyes shed tears
As each boxed the other's ears.
Each his fellow seized around,
Hurled him down onto the ground,
Where when he had got him straight,
There he banged the other's pate.
Thus they made a fearful roar
As they struggled on the floor.
Such their features' bloody sight
That I beat a hasty flight.
When I left they struggled still;
Fight, good fellows; have your fill!

This is but a tavern tale:
There no water's drunk, but ale.
Those who taverns will frequent
Often witness some event,
Or some pleasant novelty
Which one only there can see.
If to taverns you repair,
And if you will linger there,
Then you'll surely find fair matter
For your good wife's mirthful chatter,
Still it's better home to keep
And at night to have your sleep.
Let your friends their tales report,
And at home enjoy your sport.

61

PIESEŇ OD PANA ŠTEMBERKA

Račte poslúchati, co vám chci zpievati,
cot' se stalo dávno v městě v Mělníku.
Sebrali sě páni spolu měštěné.

A tut' jsú sě spolu pílně radili
a o Štemberkovi zradu skládali,
a kterak by Štemberka života zbavili.

A když jsú sě spolu pílně radili,
inhed Štemberkovi přěd sě kázali:
A poslúchaj, Štemberku, co mluví páni!

A račiž poslúchati, milý Štemberku,
co pravie páni měščěné z Mělníku,
a chceš-li ty zuostati při svém životu!

A když Štemberk to slovo zaslyšal,
inhed služebníkovi kuoň sedlat kázal:
A sedlaj ty kuoně, budeva vsědati.

THE BALLAD OF STEMBERG

Listen to my song, good folk, that you may know
What took place in Mělnik long ago.
When there gathered all the elders of the town.

Then they gathered and took counsel secretly,
And against Lord Stemberg plotted treachery:
How to take Lord Stemberg's life most faithlessly.

When the council had resolved on vengeance,
It required from Stemberg his attendance:
"Come, Lord Stemberg, for the council summons thee.

"Heed, good Stemberg, what the council orders thee,
What the citizens of Mělnik say to thee,
If thou wouldst yet dwell among the living."

And when Stemberg heard what they had now decreed,
He gave orders that his groom should saddle his swift steed:
"Saddle my good steed, for we shall ride today."

Translated
by W. E.
Harkins

63

A když Štemberk na svój kuoň vskoči,
přede pány měščěny pěknět' sě zatoči:
A buoh vy rač žehnati, milí měštěné!

A rač tě buoh žehnati, milý Štemberku!
A pospiechaj, Štemberku, z města Mělníku,
a chceš-li ty zuostati při svém životu!

A když Štemberk z brány jedieše,
jeho pěkná Anička v uokenci stojieše
a tak velmi srdečně jest zaplakala.

A rač tě buoh žehnati, má milá Aničko!
A žehnaj tě milý buoh, muoj milý Štemberku!
A komužs mě poručil, smutnú dievčičku?

A když Štemberk v pole jedieše,
inhed svému koníkovi čelo protieráše
a svá samostříly oba znapínavše.

A tut' jsú sě spolem sebrali všickni měščěné,
a o Štemberkovi zradu skládali,
a kterak by Štemberka života zbavili.

A jediný z nich vecě: Poslúchajte, páni!
A vyjed'te za ním, jměte jej na poli.
A cěle vám pravím, přídet' vám bez hanby.

A když Štemberka u poli viděli,
za ním páni měštěné hlasem volali:
A postůj, počekaj nás, Štemberku milý!

A nestřielej na nás, milý Štemberku,
však jsme my páni měštěné z Mělníku,
a však sme my páni měštěné z Mělníku.

A když jste vy páni měštěné z Mělníku,
slibujete-liž mně mému životu?
A já na vás věru střieleti nebudu.

And when Stemberg had jumped upon his steed
He caracoled and turned for all to see:
"And may God bless you all, my good townsfolk!"

"God be with thee, too, dear lord, and keep thee safe,
And a quick departure from this town vouchsafe,
If thou wouldst yet dwell among the living!"

And when Stemberg reached the gate of Mělnik town,
His fair Anna from a window did look down,
And did weep with all her heart for him.

"May God bless thee, dearest Anna, and preserve thee!"
"God bless thee, as well, dear Stemberg, and protect thee;
But to whom dost thou entrust me in my sorrow?"

When Stemberg rode across the open field,
He stroked the forehead of his fine proud steed,
And his two crossbows he made tight and fast.

And at this time all the townsmen met in secrecy,
And against Lord Stemberg plotted treachery:
How to take Lord Stemberg's life most faithlessly.

And one elder of them spoke, "Good sirs, give heed,
Let us ride out after him and take him on the mead,
For I tell you, he will yield to us and not resist!"

And when they spied Stemberk in the open field,
The Mělnik townsmen called out loud to him:
"Stand, good Lord Stemberg, wait for us, sweet sir!"

"Do not shoot at us, Lord Stemberg, as we ride;
We are honest citizens who in Mělnik town reside,
We are honest citizens who in Mělnik town reside."

"If you worthy townsmen really come in peace,
Do you promise faithfully you'll me release?
If so, then you have my word, I'll not resist."

65

A my tobě slibujem, vieru zastavujem,
že my tvému životu nic neučiníme,
že my tvému životu nic neučiníme.

A jediný sedláček, ten voral v stráni
a všecko poslúchal, co mluvie páni:
A hlédajte, páni, byste mu zdržali!

A neběhaj, Machu, muoj milý brachu,
a neboj sě sedmi pánuov strachu,
však' jest náma jindy tieže bývalo.

Jediný Kačeruov syn, ten s koně skoči,
utne Štemberkovi obě rucě, nozě.
A želiž pod klejtem, muoj milý buože!

A když Štemberka do města nesechu,
proti němu panny, panie ven vyjedechu:
A vitaj, Štemberku, náš sluho věrný!

A ja vám děkuji, panenky i panie!
Jediných sedm pánuov učinilo hnánie,
a ti jsú mě na svú čest, vieru vzali.

A tit' jsú mě na svú čest, vieru vzali,
a tak jsú mě hanebně velmi osěkali.
A želiž sě tobě, náš z Prahy králi!

A všeckot' já toto mám pro pěknú Aničku,
ještot' mi jest dala perlovú tkaničku,
a za tot' jí slúžím svú milú hlavičkú!

A ještet' já viece mám pro pannu Maruši,
a onat' mě vzala na svú milú duši,
a tak jest mě vzala na svú milú duši.

A protot' já pravím starému, mladému,
a kto kolivěk vládne u poli sám sebú:
Nedávaj sě žádný na takovú vieru.

"Yes, we promise, good Lord Stemberg, on our word,
None of us from Mělnik shall e'er draw his sword,
None of us from Mělnik shall e'er draw his sword."

And a certain peasant who was ploughing on the hill
Heard all they said and discerned they bore him ill;
"Look well, my good sirs, that you keep your word to him!"

"Do not flee, good Mach, for we shall stand our ground;
Do not fear the seven citizens of Mělnik town;
We two have been in scrapes before, my groom!"

One of Kačer's sons dismounted on the lea,
Cut off Stemberg's hands and legs most faithlessly;
Woe is us! Lord God, 'twas under oath!

When they carried Stemberg through the street,
All the ladies and the maidens gathered him to greet:
"Welcome, Stemberg, our most faithful servitor!"

"Thanks, good gentlewomen, for your grace to me,
It took seven citizens to vanquish me,
Seven townsmen who did break their oath to me!

"For those seven townsmen did break their proffered word,
And they hacked my arms and feet off with their sword;
Our lord sovereign king in Prague, oh, pity me!

"For my darling Anna they did this to me,
For that she sent a token of a pearl embroidery:
'Tis for this sin that they did this treachery.

"For Maid Mary they have done me this as well,
Who did take me on her soul in fear of hell,
Who did take me on her soul in fear of hell.

"To both young and old I counsel so:
When a man on horseback o'er a field doth go,
Let him not surrender to a faithless foe."

67

John Wickliffe, depicted in his discourse, De veritate Sacrae scripturae

68

$\mathfrak{J}$*an Hus, priest, popular preacher, graduate, later Dean and Rector, of the University of Prague, was condemned for suspected adherence to the doctrines of Wycliff, and burned for heresy at Constance in 1415. A few years later in Bohemia the Hussite rising began, its formal programme of reform based on the Four Articles of Prague. Symbols of the movement were the Chalice and the utraquist order of Communion, its centre was Tabor in Southern Bohemia. During the convulsions of the Hussite wars, the Czech people found a national identity, and embraced a Protestant ethic which was to become an enduring part of their tradition: but in the struggle the fine flower of Czech Gothic culture was destroyed. During the hard days of the battle for religious and secular freedom literature gradually lost its autonomy, becoming increasingly a vehicle for ideology, and an instrument of rhetoric and instruction. From the Hussite period there survive in the field of verse choral pieces of moral exhortation or celebration, songs of protest or satire. The following is the best-known of the Hussite battle-hymns, with it may be contrasted the satiric verses of the anti-Lollard singer.*

69

KTOŽ JSÚ BOŽÍ BOJOVNÍCI

Ktož jsú boží bojovníci
a zákona jeho,
prostež od Boha pomoci
a úfajte v něho,
že konečně vždycky s ním svítězíte!

Kristust' vám za škody stojí,
stokrat viec slibuje;
pak-li kto proň život složí,
věčný mieti bude:
blaze každému, ktož na pravdě sende.

Tent' pán velit' „se nebáti
záhubci tělesných",
velít' „i život složiti
pro lásku svých bližních".

YOU WHO ARE THE LORD'S COMBATANTS

You who are the Lord's combatants
And under his command,
Ask your God for his assistance,
Have faith in His command,
That in the end you might be victors with him.

You suffer for a worthy Christ,
He promises far more.
Those who lay down their lives for him
Have life forever more;
Happy are those men who perish for the truth.

Do not fear those who can destroy
The flesh: so God commands,
That we might give our lives in love
For friend and fellow man.

Translated
by R. G.
Vroon and
A. Levitsky

71

Protož střelci, kopiníci
řádu rytieřského,
sudličníci a cepníci
lidu rozličného,
pomnětež všichni na pána štědrého!

Nepřátel se nelekajte,
na množstvie nehled'te,
pána svého v srdci mějte,
proň a s ním bojujte
a před nepřáteli neutiekajte!

Dávno Čechové řiekali
a přislovie měli,
že „podlé dobrého pána
dobrá jiezda bývá".

Vy, pakosti a drabanti,
na duše pomněte,
pro lakomstvie a lúpeže
životóv netrat'te
a na kořistech se nezastavujte!

Heslo všichni pamatujte,
kteréž vám vydáno,
svých hauptmanóv pozorujte,
retuj druh druhého,
hlediž a drž se každý šiku svého.

A s tiem vesele křikněte
řkúc: „Na ně, hr na ně!",
braň svú rukama chutnajte,
„Bóh pán náš!" krikněte!

You archers, you who carry spears
And you of knightly rank,
You warriors armed with mace and flail,
People of every rank,
Remember God is generous and give thanks!

You who are
the Lord's
combatants

O do not fear the hostile sword
And do not count the odds;
Open your hearts before the Lord
Fight for and with your God
And do not flee before the adversary.

The Czechs of long ago would say
These words: Riding beside
A lord and master who is good
The ride is also good.

You common folk and unarmed men,
Reflect upon your souls:
Do not squander your lives in sin,
In greed and robbers' toil,
And do not stay behind for plunder and spoil!

Do not forget the battle cry
Which has been given you;
Take heed when your commanders cry,
Shield him who stands by you.
Observe your place and keep to the formation!

Then gaily shout across the land,
Against them now, hurrah! —
Clutching your weapon in your hand
Cry out, — Our Lord and God!

Eve and a snake. Litoměřice codex (1510-1514)

74

VIKLEFICE	THE LOLLARD LADY

STALA se jest příhoda
nynie tohoto hoda,
že jedna Viklefice
pozvala k sobě panice
a chtiec ho vieře naučiti,

It happened once upon a time,
Perhaps on such a holiday,
A Lollard lady called
A young lad to her side
To teach him the true faith.

Translated
by R. G.
Vroon and
A. Levitsky

a řkúc: Pro Ježíše,
příd' ke mně velmi tiše!
Chci tě vieře naučiti,
ač ty mne chceš poslúchati,
chcit' Písmo otevříti.

"Please come to me for Jesus' sake,
But come to me in silence.
I would instruct you in the faith,
And if you wish to look
I will reveal the Holy Book."

Panic Viklefce odpovědě
a na ni velmi mile hledě
řka: Já chci rád vše učiniti,
ač ty mne chceš naučiti
v tvém zákoně býti.

The lad responded to her call,
And looking on her lovingly,
He said, "I would be glad to learn
All that I must to earn
The right to join your company."

75

Vece Viklefka: Zezři na mě,
paniče, příd' ke mně
až po klidu,
když tu nebude lidu;
chcit' Písmo zjeviti.

Panic bez meškanie
učini jejie kázanie.
Po večeři v neděli,
když uhlédal svú chvíli,
přišel jest k ní tiše.

Vece Viklefice bez lenosti:
Vítaj, mój milý hosti,
co sem dávno žádala,
po němž má duše práhla!
Rač ke mně vstúpiti,

se mnú málo poseděti,
chcit' Písmo vyložiti,
biblí i také čtenie
s námat' žádného nenie,
budeš sám obierati.

Tut' mu bába biblí vyloži,
dvě kapitole vyloži
pěkné, velmi okrúhlé;
k hruškám byšta podobné
a tak velmi bílé.

Panic vece bez strachu:
Podáš jich sem, milá brachu!
Je se biblí rozkládati
a kapitol vykládati
s večera až do světu.

A když poče svítati,
panic se chtieše pryč bráti.
Viklefice se ho chváti
a řkúc: Zdet' jest ostati,
se mnú jitřni dokonati.

The lady said, "Now look at me,
My lad, come visit me
When all is still
And no one is about; I will
Reveal the Holy Book.

And so the lad without delay
Set out to follow and obey
Her words. On Sunday, after four,
He found the time to slip away
And came in silence to her door.

Eagerly the lady said,
"I welcome you, beloved guest,
You whom I have so long desired
And whom my soul has so admired,
Enter my home and rest!"

"Come sit with me a little while,
I would reveal the Word to you.
Although I have little to show
As far as books and Bibles go,
You will find things to do."

And here our Lollard lady bared
Two chapters of her Book for him,
They were so round and fair,
—Each a delicious pear—
So very pure and white.

The lad approached her without fear,
And said, "Give them to me, my dear.
The Bible should always be laid
Open, the chapters on display
From evening until morning."

When morning came at last
Our lad was set to go away;
The lady held him fast
And said, "Why don't you stay
Until we celebrate the mass?"

77

Začechu Te Deum laudamus zhóru,
jakž slušie k tomu dvoru
. . . .
. . . .
ještat' se diškantovati.

Když sú jitřni skonašta,
pěknet' se mile objašta,
v božie lásce i v milosti.
Nebylo tu nemilosti,
což mohu znamenati.

Nuž, vy mladí jinoše
i vy nádobné panoše,
kteří chcete zákon uměti,
máte se k bekyniem ptáti,
od nich se učiti.

Svědomyt' sú zákona,
Regum knih i Šalomúna,
tak Davida v žaltáři
viece než někteří faráři.
Muožte jim rádi slúžiti.

Sladkét' mají výklady,
úplné, beze všie vady.
Komut' jich dadí požíti,
muož dobře vesel býti.
Rač je, Bože, ploditi!

78

They raised a Te Deum with glee
As fits a Lollard company
. . . .
. . . .
And joined the treble clef.

When they had finished morning mass
They parted with one last embrace
In God's own love and grace.
It certainly was no disgrace,
I can attest to that!

And so, you handsome lads,
And all you fair young pages
Who wish to learn these ways,
Consult a Lollard lady
And mark well what she says.

How well she knows the rule,
The Book of Kings, the Song of Songs,
As well as David's Psalms.
She knows more than a minister,
And gladly might you wait on her.

O, her displays are ripe,
Full, round, and without flaw,
Whoever samples them has cause
To praise them joyfully.
God grant her rich fecundity!

Monks in a bath. Jena codex (1490-1510)

The emperor's court in Prague and the expanding cities of Bohemia were open to every cultural influence from Western and Southern Europe, and until the early years of the fifteenth century Czech poetry had kept pace with developments in European literature. Meanwhile a nationalist movement which was identified with the demand for religious reform had been gathering force. In the fifteenth century the Hussites and the Czech Brethren shook the established order to its foundations by their challenge to ecclesiastical authority, and by their demand for secular reorganisation to bring to birth a new society based on original Christian principles.

An ultimate effect of the Hussite movement was the diversion of cultural endeavour into the struggle for religious, ideological, and nationalist aims. The price of their success was the temporary withdrawal of the Czech intelligentsia from the mainstream of Western cultural development at the very time when the Renaissance achieved its maximum impact on Western Europe. The fifteenth century is not a good period for Czech poetry: of the verse which survives the most noteworthy is devoted to spiritual themes, much of it still filled with the spirit of the old medieval world. The following poem, typical of its kind and time, is taken from the collection of the Utraquist priest Václav Miřinský, who died in 1492.

81

Václav
Miřinský

ACH MŮJ SMUTKU

Ach můj smutku, má žalosti,
nemohu mít vědomosti,
kde můj první nocleh bude,
když tělo duše pozbude.

V rozkošech z mladosti jsem byl,
duše sobě nic nevážil,
již stůni, maje umříti,
duše, nevím, kde má jíti.

Co jsem měl statku ve dvoře,
v truhlách, v skrejších i v komoře,
to vše musím opustiti,
nikdá se nenavrátiti.

Dítky s matkou naříkají,
bratří na očisto lkají,
k nápadu se přiblížují,
o duši mou nepečují.

Ach, ach! procítiž duše má,
probudiž se rychle ze sna,
nenajdeš věrného tobě,
učiniž dnes dobře sobě.

Podvodný svět mne zklamával,
dlouhý cíl žití pokládal,
včera nemoh jsem mysliti,
abych již dnes měl umříti.

Síla má, nadělání mé,
den po dni pracně nabyté,
kam se jen poděje? V hrobě
plátna kousek mám na sobě.

82

MY SORROW

Translated
by Alfred
French

Sad and cheerless is the anguish
Haunting my uncertain heart;
What first resting place awaits me
When my soul and body part?

Young, I heeded not the spirit,
Worldly follies filled my day.
Sick and dying now, I know not
Where my soul must flit away.

All the goods within my household,
garnered treasures, gathered store,
Everything I must abandon,
I will never see them more.

Weeping mother, children, brothers,
Raise their voice in mournful dole,
Closing in to take the pickings;
Little care they for my soul.

Waken, O my soul, awaken!
Now the time for dreams is gone,
Not one faithful mourner tarries:
Now, my soul, your hour has come.

Vain and false, the world deceived me;
Trusting to this mortal clay
Yesterday I could not credit
Death will come for me today.

All my work and all my effort,
Day by day the strength I gave,
Whither fled? — but this is left me —
Rags to shroud me in the grave.

Peníze jsem shromažd'oval,
tělo své v rozkoši choval
po všecky dni věku svého,
nectil jsem dne svátečního.

Almužny jsem nerad dával,
Bohu neobětovával,
prvních i druhých obětí
nemíval jsem na paměti.

Tak jsem býval velmi hloupý,
jiným štědrý, sobě skoupý,
sliby Bohu učiněné
ode mne nejsou plněné.

Ležíc tělo, velmi chřádne,
duše zase strachem vadne,
Pan Bůh z počtu upomíná:
d'ábel hříchy připomíná.

Smrt svým šípem prsy leká,
duše z těla nepospíchá,
vidí peklo otevřené,
i nebe také zavřené.

Musím již dnes z zadu jíti,
nelze se před Bohem skrýti,
lépe na světě nebýti,
nežli věčné peklo míti.

Ó dušičko, drahý květe,
nic dražšího nad tě v světě:
v tom jsi d'áblu se prodala,
žes hříchy hrozné páchala.

Vzpomeň, cos na křtu slíbila,
tos vše bídně přestoupila,
odřeklas se d'ábla zlého,
pejchy, lakomství škodného.

Greedily I piled up riches,
Trod the devil's sinful ways,
Day by day in Mammon's service,
Breaking Heaven's Holy days.

Alms I gave reluctantly,
Little in God's service spent:
Sacrifice to man or heaven,
All were far from my intent.

Stinting self I gave to others,
Folly was my constant sin.
Promises to God I offered,
Then I broke my vows to Him.

Prostrate body — sick and sinking —
Soul in mortal fear downcast;
God — the voice of retribution;
Satan — of my sinful past.

Death takes aim. The soul recoiling
To the body clings aghast:
Fearful sight of hell's mouth gaping,
Heaven's portals shuttered fast.

This day I must face my judgement,
No escape remains for me.
Better never taste existence
Than to burn eternally.

O my spirit, precious flower,
God's most precious gift to man,
By my deadly sins I lost you,
Sold you to the Evil One.

Promises you made at baptism
Wretchedly you did transgress;
Then you vowed to put behind you
Pride and greed and wickedness.

85

Pospěš již rychle k zpovědi,
kněz, žádej, ať tě navštíví:
želej hříchu, přijmi svátost,
plač hořce, ať padne tvá zlost.

Rolí s domem dítkám oddej,
nadělání chudým rozdej,
z statku přátel nabývaje,
vpravíš duši svou do ráje.

Shromažd' dělníky, dlužníky:
odpust', zaplat' dluh všeliký,
netrat' duše ani dětí,
nechceš-li v pekle hořeti.

Nyní tam duše má vzhlídá,
duchů nesčíslnou moc vídá,
leká se: zlé zpomínají
hříchy, léčky zakládají.

Vrtí se, pomoci hledá,
hrdla za ni žádný nedá,
naděje v přátelích není,
jen v Bohu: ten se nemění.

Kriste, pro tvé umučení,
rozžen d'áblů pokušení,
dej mi svaté požehnání
a těla lehké skonání.

Já jsem tvůj syn, ač pak hříšný,
tys můj otec milosrdný,
lituji, že jsem kdy hněval
tebe, zlému nevyhejbal.

Rozžetež mi svíci směle,
moji přemilí přátelé,
duše jde s potem krvavým,
mně dnes, zejtra vám, tot' pravím.

Quickly hasten to confession,
Call the priest, together pray!
Take the Host in true repentance:
Tears will wash your sins away.

Home and fields donate to children,
Shower largesse upon the poor!
Gather friends, instead of riches:
Heaven's salvation will be sure.

Call together servants, debtors;
Pay each due, remit each fee.
Wish no harm on child or spirit,
Save your soul from purgatory.

Now I glimpse the ghostly legion,
Terrified my soul recoils.
Dread reminders of my sinning
lure her on toward the toils.

In each face she seeks salvation,
Everywhere to no avail.
Not in friends lies hope of rescue,
Only God! He does not fail.

For Thy sacred Passion, Jesu,
Grant from Satan's power release!
Give Thy servant holy blessing;
Let my soul depart in peace!

Thou art my forgiving Father,
I, though sinful, yet Thy son,
Mourning that I moved Thy anger,
listened to the Evil One.

Resolutely light the candle
Over me, my comrades true!
Painfully the soul is passing,
I today — tomorrow you!

87

CHVÁLA MOUDROSTI

Tomáš Rešel
Hradecký
(1557)

MOUDROST chváliti bude duši svou
   a v Pánu Bohu uctěna bude,
   a v prostředku lidu svého chlubiti se bude . . .
Já z oust Nejvyššího pošla jsem,
   prvorozená před všelikým stvořením.
Já jsem učinila at'by na nebi vycházelo světlo neskonalé
   a jako mlhou přikryla jsem všecknu zemi.
Já na výsostech přebývala jsem
   a stolice má na sloupě oblakovém.
Okršlek nebeský obešla jsem sama
   a hlubokost propasti pronikla,
   a po vlnobití mořském chodila,
   a na všeliké zemi stála jsem . . .
Od počátku a před věky stvořena jsem
   a až do budoucího věku nezhynu.
Jako cedr povýšena jsem na hoře libánské
   a jako cypřiš na hoře syonské.
Jako palma vyvýšena jsem v Kades
   a jako štípení růže v Jerycho.
Jako oliva krásná na poli
   a jako javor vyvýšena jsem
   podlé vod na ulicích.
Jako skořice a balsam vonný vydala jsem vůni
   a jako mirra výborná dala jsem chutnost vůně.
A jako storax a galban a ungula a gutta
   a jako dřevo libánské nepodt'até
   učinila jsem vonný příbytek můj
   a jako balsam nesmíšený vůně má.
Já jako smrk rozložila jsem ratolesti mé
   a větve mé jsou cti a milosti.
Já jako vinný kořen zplodila jsem chutnou vůni
   a kvítí mé ovotce cti a poctivosti.
Já matka krásného milováni
   i bázně i poznání a svaté naděje.

PRAISE TO WISDOM

WISDOM shall praise her spirit
    and be esteemed in the Lord God,
    and shall glory in the midst of her people . . .
I came forth from the mouth of the All Highest,
    first-born before all creation.
I willed a mighty radiance to rise up in the skies
    and as with mist I covered the whole earth.
I dwelt in the high places,
    my throne on a pillar of clouds.
The circuit of heavens I compassed alone
    and pierced the depths of the abyss,
    and walked on the waves of the sea,
    and on every land I was established . . .
From the beginning and before the ages, I was created,
    and to the end of time I shall not fail.
Like a cedar I was exalted on the mountain of Lebanon,
    like a cypress on Mount Sinai.
Like a palm tree I soared in Kades,
    like a rose bush in Jericho.
Like a graceful olive upon the plain,
    like a maple I soared
    beside the waters in the streets.
Like cinnamon and scented balsam did I spread my fragrance,
    like choice myrrh I gave forth fragrant scent.
Like storax and galban and ungula and gutta,
    like an untouched tree of Lebanon,
    I made fragrant my tabernacle:
    and as pure balsam is my fragrance.
Like a spruce I stretched out my branches,
    and my shoots are the branches of honor and grace.
I, like the root of the vine, put forth delicious fragrance,
    and my flowers are the fruits of honor and righteousness.
I am the mother of decorous loving,
    of fear, of knowledge, of holy faith.

Translated
by A.
Levitsky

Ve mně všeliká milost života a pravdy
   a ve mně všeliká naděje života a ctnosti.
Pojd'te ke mně všickni, kteříž žádáte mne
   a od zplození mých naplněni bud'te.
Duch zajisté můj sladký jest nad med
   a dědictvi mé nad plást strdi.
Památka má v pokolení věkův,
   kdo mne jedí, ještě lačněti budou,
   a kdož mne pijí, ještět' žízniti budou.
Kdo slyší mne nebude pohanín,
   a kteříž pracují ve mně nebudout' hřešiti,
   kteříž vypravují mne život věčný míti budou.
Uložil Davidovi, služebníku svému,
   zbuditi krále z něho nejsilnějšího
   a na stolici cti sedícího na věky.
Kterýž naplňuje jako potok rajský Fizon
   moudrostí všecky věci
   a jako Týgrys ve dnech nových úrod.
Kterýž naplňuje jako Eufrates rozum,
   kterýž rozmnožuje jako Jordán v čas žní.
Kterýž posílá kázeň jako světlo
   a přístojí jako potok rajský Gion
   v den zbírání vína.
Kterýž dokonává, aby první uměl ji,
   a mdlejši nedosáhne jí.
Nebo od moře rozmnoži se myšlení její
   a rada její v propasti veliké.
Já moudrost vylila jsem řeky,
   já jsem jako zátoka vody nesmírné z řeky.
Ja jako potok Doryx
   a jako vedení vody vyplynula jsem z ráje.
Řekla jsem: svlažím zahradu štěpovou
   a naplním dědiny mé ovotcem.
A hle, učinila mi se zátoka hojná
   a potok můj přiblížil se k moři.
Nebo naučení jako svítaní osvětluji všechněm
   a budu vypravovati je až na kraj světa.
Proniknu všecky nižší strany země
   a shlédnu všecky, kteříž spí
   a osvítím všecky doufající v Pána Boha.

In me is all grace of life and of truth
   in me is all hope of life and of righteousness.
Come unto me all ye who desire me
   and be filled with my offspring.
Truly is my spirit sweeter than honey,
   and my inheritance beyond the sweetness of combs.
The memory of me is in the generations of ages,
   they that eat of me shall hunger for more,
   they that drink of me shall yet feel thirst.
They that hearken unto me shall not be pagans;
   and they that work in me shall not transgress:
   they that walk in my ways will have life everlasting.
He appointed his servant David
   to become the mightiest of kings,
   sitting upon the throne of honor unto eternity.
It is He fills all things with Wisdom
   as Fizon, the stream of paradise
   as the Tigris in the days of new fruits.
He makes full the understanding, as the Euphrates;
   He multiplies, as the Jordan at the time of harvest.
He sends his commandment to shine like a light
   as Gion, the stream of paradise, He stands,
   on the day of the vintage.
He makes the first man to know her,
   nor shall the weaker attain her.
For her thoughts are multiplied from the sea
   and her counsel in the great deep.
I, Wisdom, have poured forth rivers,
   I am as a pool of water from a mighty river.
I am like the stream Doryx,
   like a conduit I flowed out of paradise.
I said: I will water my garden
   and will fill my homeland with fruits.
And lo, my pool became abundant,
   and my stream became as a sea.
Like the sunrise I will make my doctrine shine forth to all men
   and will send it forth to the limits of the world.
I shall penetrate unto the lower reaches of the earth,
   and will look on all who sleep,
   and will shine on all who trust in the Lord God.

91

CHVÁLA BOHA Z KRÁSY NEBES
A TVORŮ

Tomáš Rešel
Hradecký
(1557)

OBLOHA výsosti nebeské jestiť krása boží,
ozdoba nebeská jestiť spatření slávy.
Slunce zvěstuje světlo při svém východu
a jest nádoba divná, dílo Nejvyššiho.
O poledni páli zemi a proti horkosti jeho
kdo bude moci ostáti?
Jako třikrát více nežli pec maje v sobě horkost
slunce vypaluje hory,
paprslky ohnivé vypouštěje
a blýskaje jimi zaslepuje oči.
Veliký Pán, kterýž stvořil je
a k slovu jeho pospichá cestou svou.
MĚSÍC při všech věcech časem svým
jeť vyměřováním času a znamení věků
Od měsíce jest znamení dne svátečního,
světlo, kteréž se umenšuje na skonání.
Měsíc slove jméno jeho, že se obnovuje,
divně se mění až do skonání.
Způsoba vojenská HVĚZD jest na výsostech
a na obloze nebeské stkví se slavně.
Okrasa nebe jest z slávy hvězd,
svět osvěcuje na výsostech Pán.
K slovům svatým jeho stojí v svém pořádku
a neustávají v práci své.
Pohleď na DUHU a pochval toho,
kterýž ji učinil,
kterak velmi krásná jeť v blesku svém.
Obklíčila nebe v okršlku slávy své,
ruce Nejvyššiho roztáhly ji.
Rozkázáním svým dal s nebe sníh,
pospíšil vydati blýskání soudu svého.
Protož otevříni jsou pokladové
a vyšly mlhy jako ptáci.
V velikosti své položil oblaky
a zetříno jest kamení krupobití.

PRAISE TO GOD FOR THE BEAUTY OF HEAVENS
AND LIVING CREATURES

The firmament of heaven's height is the beauty of God,
the adornment of heaven is the spectacle of glory.
The SUN at his rising heralds the light,
and is a wondrous vessel, the work of the Most High.
At mid-day it scorches the earth, and against its heat
what man shall avail?
Its heat exceeds threefold the hottest oven;
the sun parches the mountains,
breathing out fiery rays
whose brilliance dims men's eyes.
Great is the Lord who created it,
and according to His word it hastens on its course.
The MOON in all things in her season
is for a measuring of time, and a sign of ages.
From the moon is the sign of feast-day,
a light that wanes unto vanishing.
The month preserves her name, because she renews herself,
strangely she changes unto vanishing.
A legion of STARS is in the heights,
and in the firmament of heaven they shine in glory.
An adornment of heaven is the glory of stars;
in the heights the Lord casts radiance upon the world.
At His holy word they stand arrayed,
and faint not in their endeavour.
Behold the RAINBOW, and praise the One
Who made it,
exceeding beautiful in the brightness thereof.
It encompassed the sky in the circle of its glory,
the hands of the Most High did bend it.
By His commandment He made the snow to fall from heaven,
and swiftly He sent the lightning of his judgement.
By reason thereof the treasure-houses were opened
and mists came forth like the birds of the air.
In His might He condensed the clouds
and the hail stones were broken small.

From the
Apocrypha:
Ekk. XLIII
Translated
by A.
Levitsky
and A.
French

Před obličejem jeho zatřesou se hory
  a k vůli jeho pověje vítr polední.
  Zvuk hřímáni jeho obráží zemi,
  bouře půlnoční i shromáždění větrův.
A jako pták spouštěje křídla k sedění sype sněhem.
  a jako kobylky spadající k zemi,
  tak jest padání jeho:
  pěknosti bělosti jeho diviti se bude oko
  a přivalu jeho ulekne se srdce.
Mráz jako sůl posype na zemi
  a když zmrzne bude jako vrch bodlákový.
  Studený vítr vál od půlnoci
  i zmrzla voda co křišťál,
  nad každým shromážděním vod odpočívá
  a jako v pancíř obláčí vody.
  A požře hory, vypálí poušť
  a usuší zelenost jako oheň.
Lékařství všechněm věcem v přicházeni mlhy
  a rosa horkost přílíšnou přicházející svlaží.
  V řečí boží utišil se vítr,
  pomyšlením jeho ukrotila se propast
  a stvořil ji Pán Jezus.
Kteříž se plaví přes moře,
  tit' vypravuji nebezpečenství jeho,
  a my slyšíce ušima našima, diviti se budeme.
  Tam jsou překrásní skutkové,
  divná a rozličná pokolení šelm
  i všech hovad a stvoření potvor.
Pro něho utvrzen jest konec cesty
  a v řeči jeho zřízeny jsou všeckny věci.
  Mnohé věci pravíme a nedostává se nám slov,
  ale skonání řečí, ont' jest ve všech věcech.
Chlubíce se, jací budeme?
  neb on zajisté všemohoucí jest
  nade všeckny skutky své.
  Hrozný Pán a veliký příliš
  a divná moc jeho.

Before His face the mountains tremble,
and at His will the south wind blows.
The sound of His thunder shakes the earth,
and the northern storm and the whirlwind.
As a bird spreading its wings to alight, He sends the snow,
and as locusts descending to earth;
even so is the falling thereof.
The eye will marvel at the beauty of its whiteness
the heart will tremble at its falling.
Frost He sprinkles upon the earth like salt,
and when it is congealed it will be as points of thorns.
The cold wind blew from the north
and the water was frozen as crystal;
upon every pool of water it abides,
and clothes them as in armour.
It will devour mountains, parch the desert,
and dry the green herb like fire.
A healing of all things is in the coming of mist,
and the dew at its coming refreshes the scorching heat.
In the word of God the storm is hushed,
by His counsel the deep is stilled,
and the Lord Jesus created it.
Those who travel upon the sea
they tell of the dangers thereof;
and hearkening with our ears, we shall marvel.
Therein are wondrous works,
strange and varied generations of beasts,
of all animals and monsters created.
For His sake the end of the journey is fixed,
and in His word are all things made firm.
We say many things, and our words fall short;
but the sum of our utterance is: He is all.
In glorification, what shall be our quality?
for He is in truth the Almighty,
standing above all His works.
The Lord is terrible, and exceeding great,
and marvellous in His power.

Slavte Pána Boha jakžkoli můžete,
   ještět' jest on vždy vyšší
   a předivná velebnost jeho.
Chvalte Pána Boha, vyvyšujte ho jakž můžete,
   však on jest ještě větší chvály hodný.
   Vyvyšujíce ho naplněni buďte mocí,
   neusilujte dokonale ho poznati,
   neb nedosáhnete.
Kdož uhlídá ho a bude vypravovati vo něm?
   A kdo jej zvelebí tak, jako jest od počátku?
   Mnohé zajisté věci skryté jsou,
   větší nežli jsú tyto,
   neb málo viděli jsme skutkův a díla jeho.
Všecky zajisté věci Pán Bůh učinil
   a dobře činícím dal MOUDROST.

Glorify the Lord God as ye may,
yet will your words ever fall short:
wonderful is His majesty.
Praise ye the Lord God, exalt Him as ye may,
yet is He ever worthy of greater praise.
Exalting Him, be ye filled with power,
yet strive not to see Him entire,
for ye will not attain.
Who can perceive Him, that he may declare Him?
And who shall magnify Him, even as He has been from the
                                            beginning?

Surely there are many things hidden
that are greater than these;
for we have seen but few of His works and of His creation.
Verily the Lord God hath made all things,
and to the godly hath he imparted WISDOM

Initial P in "Píseň písní" ("The Song of Songs") Bible kralická (16th century)

hristian lore and holy celebration are a theme for the earliest surviving documents of Czech literature: it drew artistic, as well as religious, inspiration from translations of the Hebrew sacred classics, which thereby became a part of the Czech literary heritage. At the end of the XVI century a complete collection of the biblical books was published in the Kralická Bible, whose quality and authority made it long a pattern for elevated Czech literary style. Below is a facsimile of the Song of Songs, that great model for lyrics of sacred and profane love.

99

 Jseň [z gi-
nych] pjsnj Ssa-
lomaunowých[a].

2 O by mne polj-
bil[b] poljbenjm vst
swých: nebo le-
pssi gsau miłosti
twé, nežli wjno[c].

3 Pro samu wůni, masti twé gsau wybor-
né/ nýbrž gako mast rozlitá gméno twé:
protož tě mladice milugj[d].

4 Tahniž mne[e]/ a takě zatebau pobě-
hnem[f]. Vwedltě mne giž Král[g] do poko-
gů swých[h]/protož plésati a weseliti se w tobě budeme[i]/a [k]wychwalowati miłosti twé
wjce nežli wjno: nebo [l]vpřjmj milugj tě.

5 Gsemť černá[m]/ale [n]miłostná/ ó dcery
Geruzalémské/tak gako stanowé Cedar-
stj/ gako opony[o] Ssalomaunowy.

6 A protož nehleďte namne[p]/žeť sem sně-
dá

THE SONG OF SOLOMON

THE SONG

OF SONGS,

WHICH IS SOLOMON'S.

2 LET HIM KISS ME

WITH THE KISSES OF HIS MOUTH:

FOR THY LOVE

IS BETTER THAN WINE.

3 BECAUSE OF THE SAVOUR OF THY GOOD OINTMENTS

THY NAME IS AS OINTMENT POURED FORTH,

THEREFORE DO THE VIRGINS LOVE THEE.

4 DRAW ME, WE WILL RUN AFTER THEE:

THE KING HATH BROUGHT ME INTO HIS CHAMBERS:

WE WILL BE GLAD AND REJOICE IN THEE,

WE WILL REMEMBER THY LOVE MORE THAN WINE:

THE UPRIGHT LOVE THEE.

5 I AM BLACK, BUT COMELY,

O YE DAUGHTERS OF JERUSALEM,

AS THE TENTS OF KEDAR, AS THE CURTAINS OF SOLOMON.

6 LOOK NOT UPON ME, BECAUSE I AM BLACK,

dá: nebo ᵃſem obhořela od ſlunce: ktomu,
ſynowé matky méᵏ rozpáliwſſe ſe proti
mně/ poſtawili mne abych oſtřjhala wi‑
nic/geſſto gá winice ſwé kterauž ſem měla
oſtřjhatibych nemohla⁵.

7 Oznamᵗ mi, ty kteréhož miluge duſſe
má, kde paſeš:ᵖkde dáwáš odpocžinutj dobyt
ku opoledníᵘ:ᵖnebo procž mám býtiᵐtak ga
ko ᵣpoběhlá při ſtádjch towaryſſů twých ᵛ.

8   ᶜGeſtliže newjšˢ, ó neykraſſſj ze
wſſech žen / wygdiᵘ a beř ſe po ſſlepégjch
ᵇowcý/a pasᶜ kozlátka ſwá podlé ᵈobydlj
giných paſtýřůw.

9 ᵗᵉGjzdě w wozých Faraonowých při‑
podobňugi tě, ó miloſtnice má :

10 Vſſlechtiletᵉ gſau okráſſlena ljce twá
ozdobami/ a hrdlo twé ᶠhalžemi:

11 Ozdob zlatých naděláme ᵍ tobě sʰpro‑
měnami ſtřjbrnými.

12   ᶜᵗDotud dokudž král ſtolj/ nardus
můg wydáwá wůni ſwauⁱ:

BECAUSE THE SUN HATH LOOKED UPON ME:

MY MOTHER'S CHILDREN WERE ANGRY WITH ME;

THEY MADE ME THE KEEPER OF THE VINEYARDS;

BUT MINE OWN VINEYARD HAVE I NOT KEPT.

7 TELL ME, O THOU WHOM MY SOUL LOVETH,

WHERE THOU FEEDEST,

WHERE THOU MAKEST THY FLOCK TO REST AT NOON:

FOR WHY SHOULD I BE AS ONE

THAT TURNETH ASIDE BY THE FLOCKS OF THY COMPANIONS?

8 IF THOU KNOW NOT, O THOU FAIREST AMONG WOMEN,

GO THY WAY FORTH BY THE FOOTSTEPS OF THE FLOCK,

AND FEED THY KIDS BESIDE THE SHEPHERDS' TENTS.

9 I HAVE COMPARED THEE, O MY LOVE,

TO A COMPANY OF HORSES IN PHARAOH'S CHARIOTS.

10 THY CHEEKS ARE COMELY WITH ROWS OF JEWELS,

THY NECK WITH CHAINS OF GOLD.

11 WE WILL MAKE THEE BORDERS OF GOLD WITH STUDS OF SILVER.

12 WHILE THE KING SITTETH AT HIS TABLE,

MY SPIKENARD SENDETH FORTH THE SMELL THEREOF.

13 Miſto [k]ſwazečku mirry, geſt mi milý
můg, na prſech mých odpočjwage[l]:
14 Milý můg geſt mi gako hrozen[m] †cy-
prowý na winnicých w Engády[n].
15 ¶ Ay gak gſy ty kráſná, přjtelkyně[o] má
ay gak gſy kráſná! oči twé gako holubičj[p]
16 ¶ Ay gak gſy ty kráſný milý můg / gak
vtěſſený! y to lůže náſſe geſt zelenagjcý ſe[q]
17 Trámowé domůw naſſich gſau z ce-
dru / [r]pawlače náſſe z dřjwj borowého[s].

Kapitola II.

JA gſem gako růže Sáronſká[a] /
a gako lilium [b]při dolinách:
2 Gako lilium mezy trnjm, [c]tak
přjtelkyně má mezy[d] pannami.
3 † ¶ Gako gabloň mezy dřjwjm leſnjm[e] /
tak milý můg mezy [f]mládency: w ſtjnu
geho žádoſtiwa ſem byla ſeděti[g] / a ſedjm:
nebo owoce geho ſladké geſt vſtům mým.

13 A BUNDLE OF MYRRH IS MY WELL-BELOVED UNTO ME;

HE SHALL LIE ALL NIGHT BETWIXT MY BREASTS.

14 MY BELOVED IS UNTO ME AS A CLUSTER OF CAMPHIRE

IN THE VINEYARDS OF ENGEDI.

15 BEHOLD, THOU ART FAIR, MY LOVE;

BEHOLD, THOU ART FAIR; THOU HAST DOVES' EYES.

16 BEHOLD, THOU ART FAIR, MY BELOVED,

YEA, PLEASANT: ALSO OUR BED IS GREEN.

17 THE BEAMS OF OUR HOUSE ARE CEDAR,

AND OUR RAFTERS OF FIR.

CHAPTER 2

I AM THE ROSE OF SHARON, AND THE LILY OF THE VALLEYS.

2 AS THE LILY AMONG THORNS,

SO IS MY LOVE AMONG THE DAUGHTERS.

3 AS THE APPLE TREE AMONG THE TREES OF THE WOOD,

SO IS MY BELOVED AMONG THE SONS.

I LAY DOWN UNDER HIS SHADOW WITH GREAT DELIGHT,

AND HIS FRUIT WAS SWEET TO MY TASTE.

4 Vwedł mne "na hody/ 'mage za ko-
rauhew láſku ke mné.

5 'Očerſtwétež mne témi ſflaſſemi'/"po-
ſylíte mne témi gablky";nebo °vmdléwám
miloſtj.

6 'Lewice geho geſt pod hlawau mau'/
a prawicý ſwau obgjmá mne.

7 'Zawazugič'wás přjſahau dcery Ge-
ruzalémſké,ſkrze ſrny a lané polnj'/abyſſte
nebudiły, a newyrážeły zeſna 'miléhо mého'/dokudžby ſám nechtěł.

8 'Hlas miléhо méhо ſkyſſim/ ay onť ſe
béře': ſkáce" po těch horách: poſkakuge
na těch pahrbcých:

9 Podobný geſt milý můg ſrně"/a neb
'mladému gelenu: ay on ſtogj za ſtěnau
naſſj': wyhlédá z oken: 'patřj ſkrze mřjžj.

10 Anobrž ozwal ſe milý můg, a řekł mi;
"Wſtaň přjtelkyně má, kráſná má/a pod.

11 Nebo ay zyma pominula'/prſſka pře-
ſtala, a'odeſſla:

12 Kwjtjčko ſe vkazuge po zemi: čas
pro-

106

4 HE BROUGHT ME TO THE BANQUETING HOUSE,

AND HIS BANNER OVER ME WAS LOVE.

5 STAY ME WITH FLAGONS, COMFORT ME WITH APPLES:

FOR I AM SICK OF LOVE.

6 HIS LEFT HAND IS UNDER MY HEAD,

AND HIS RIGHT HAND DOTH EMBRACE ME.

7 I CHARGE YOU, O YE DAUGHTERS OF JERUSALEM, BY THE ROES,

AND BY THE HINDS OF THE FIELD, THAT YE STIR NOT UP,

NOR AWAKE MY LOVE, TILL HE PLEASE.

8 THE VOICE OF MY BELOVED! BEHOLD,

HE COMETH LEAPING UPON THE MOUNTAINS,

SKIPPING UPON THE HILLS.

9 MY BELOVED IS LIKE A ROE OR A YOUNG HART:

BEHOLD, HE STANDETH BEHIND OUR WALL,

HE LOOKETH FORTH AT THE WINDOWS,

SHEWING HIMSELF THROUGH THE LATTICE.

10 MY BELOVED SPAKE, AND SAID UNTO ME,

RISE UP, MY LOVE, MY FAIR ONE, AND COME AWAY.

11 FOR, LO, THE WINTER IS PAST, THE RAIN IS OVER AND GONE;

THE FLOWERS APPEAR ON THE EARTH;

107

[o]prozpěwowánj přiſſel / a hlas hrdličky
ſlyſſj ſe w kragině naſſj :
13 Fjk wypuſtil [e]holičky ſwé / a réwj [f]roz-
kwetlé wydalo wůni[g] : †wſtaniž přjtelkyně
má / kráſná ma / a pod :
14 †Holubičko má[h] / genž přebýwáš w roz-
ſedlinách ſkalnjch[i], w ſkreyſſi [k]přjkré : vkaž
mi obljčeg ſwůg[l] : †nechať ſlyſſjm hlas
twůg : nebo hlas twůg libý geſt[m] / a obljčeg twůg žádoſtiwý.
15 †Rekl y to ; Zlapeyte nám liſſky / liſſky
prawjm y ty maličké[n] / geſſto ſſkodu dělagj
na winicech / poněwadž winice náſſe teprw
kwete.
16 † Milý můg, geſt můg / a gá geho[o] /
genž paſe[p] ſtádo ſwé mezy lilium.
17 †Ažby[q] zawjtal ten den[r] / a vtekliby
ſtjnowé ti[s], nawratiž ſe[t] : připodobni ſe
milý můg †ſrně / neb mladému gelenu, bě-
hagjcýmu na horách †Beter.

Kapitola III.

THE TIME OF THE SINGING OF BIRDS IS COME,

AND THE VOICE OF THE TURTLE IS HEARD IN OUR LAND;

13 THE FIG TREE PUTTETH FORTH HER GREEN FIGS, AND

THE VINES WITH THE TENDER GRAPE GIVE A GOOD SMELL

ARISE, MY LOVE, MY FAIR ONE, AND COME AWAY.

14 O MY DOVE, THAT ART IN THE CLEFTS OF THE ROCK,

IN THE SECRET PLACES OF THE STAIRS,

LET ME SEE THY COUNTENANCE, LET ME HEAR THY VOICE;

FOR SWEET IS THY VOICE, AND THY COUNTENANCE IS COMELY.

15 TAKE US THE FOXES, THE LITTLE FOXES, THAT SPOIL THE VINES:

FOR OUR VINES HAVE TENDER GRAPES.

16 MY BELOVED IS MINE, AND I AM HIS;

HE FEEDETH AMONG THE LILIES.

17 UNTIL THE DAY BREAK, AND THE SHADOWS FLEE AWAY,

TURN, MY BELOVED, AND BE THOU LIKE A ROE

OR A YOUNG HART UPON THE MOUNTAINS OF BETHER.

CHAPTER 3

A ložcy swém ᵃw nocy hledala sem toho kteréhož miluge dusse má: hledala sem ho/ ale nenassla sem hoᵇ:

2ᵈᶻ řekla sem; Gižť wstanu / a zchodjmᶜ město:po ryňcých y po vlicechᵈ hledati budu toho, kteréhož miluge dusse má: ᵉhledala sem ho/ale nenassla sem ho.

3 ᶠwtom nassli mne ponocnjᵉ, kteřjž chodj po městě/ y řekla sem gimᶠ; Widěliližste toho, kteréhož miluge dusse má:ᶻ

4 A gakž sem gich gen pominula/ takž sem nassla toho kteréhož miluge dusse má: chopila sem ho/ aniž ho pustjmᵍ/ až ho vwedu do domuʰ matky swé/a do pokogjka rodičky swé.

5 ᶜ:Přjsahau wás zawazugi dcery Gerusalémské, skrze srny a lané polnj/ abysste nebudily, a newyrážely ze sna ᵢmilého mého, dokudžby sám nechtěl.

6ᵏKterá gest to genž wstupuge z pausstě'/ gako ᵢslaupowé dymuᵐ/ okaučena gsuc mirrau a kadidlem drazssjm nad wsseligaký prach ⁿApatekářský.

, ¹ᵒ Ey lože' Ssalomaunowo /okolo néhož stogj ssedesáte vdatných reků, z neysylnégssjch Jzraelskýchᵍ/

110

BY NIGHT ON MY BED I SOUGHT HIM WHOM MY SOUL LOVETH:

I SOUGHT HIM, BUT I FOUND HIM NOT.

2 I WILL RISE NOW AND GO ABOUT THE CITY IN THE STREETS,

AND IN THE BROAD WAYS I WILL SEEK HIM

WHOM MY SOUL LOVETH: I SOUGHT HIM,

BUT I FOUND HIM NOT.

3 THE WATCHMEN THAT GO ABOUT THE CITY FOUND ME:

TO WHOM I SAID, SAW YE HIM WHOM MY SOUL LOVETH?

4 IT WAS BUT A LITTLE THAT I PASSED FROM THEM,

BUT I FOUND HIM WHOM MY SOUL LOVETH:

I HELD HIM, AND WOULD NOT LET HIM GO,

UNTIL I HAD BROUGHT HIM INTO MY MOTHER'S HOUSE,

AND INTO THE CHAMBER OF HER THAT CONCEIVED ME.

5 I CHARGE YOU, O YE DAUGHTERS OF JERUSALEM,

BY THE ROES, AND BY THE HINDS OF THE FIELD,

THAT YE STIR NOT UP, NOR AWAKE MY LOVE, TILL HE PLEASE.

6 WHO IS THIS THAT COMETH OUT OF THE WILDERNESS

LIKE PILLARS OF SMOKE, PERFUMED WITH MYRRH

AND FRANKINCENSE, WITH ALL POWDERS OF THE MERCHANT?

7 BEHOLD HIS BED, WHICH IS SOLOMON'S;

THREE SCORE VALIANT MEN ARE ABOUT IT, OF THE VALIANT OF
ISRAEL.

8 Wſſe mužůw wkládnaucých mečem, wycwičených w bogi / z nichž geden každý má ſwůg meč při boku ſwém, z přjčiny ſtrachu nočnjho.

9 'Pokog také wyſtawěl ſobě král Ssalomaun z dřjwj Libánſkého,

10 W kterémžto nadělal ſlaupůw ſtřjbrných : w němž poſtawil poſtel zlatau / na njž 'ſſaty ložnj ſſarlatowé / a kteráž wnitř geſt poſtlána miloſtj dcer Geruzalémſkých.

11 Wygděte, a pohleſſteᵗ dcery Syonſké na krále Ssalomauna / w koruně kterauž ho korunowala "matka geho, w den od dáwánj geho / a w den weſelj ſrdce geho.

Kapitola IIII.

AX' gak gſy ty kráſná přjtelkyně má ! ay gak gſy kráſná ! *očiᶻtwé gako holubičj, mezy kadeři twými" : ⁶wlaſy twé gako ſtáda koz, kteréž wjdati na hoře Galád.

2 'Zubowé twogi podobnj ſtádu owcý

112

8 THEY ALL HOLD SWORDS, BEING EXPERT IN WAR:

EVERY MAN HATH HIS SWORD UPON HIS THIGH

BECAUSE OF FEAR IN THE NIGHT.

9 KING SOLOMON MADE HIMSELF

A CHARIOT OF THE WOOD OF LEBANON.

10 HE MADE THE PILLARS THEREOF OF SILVER, THE BOTTOM

THEREOF OF GOLD, THE COVERING OF IT OF PURPLE,

THE MIDST THEREOF BEING PAVED WITH LOVE,

FOR THE DAUGHTERS OF JERUSALEM.

11 GO FORTH, O YE DAUGHTERS OF ZION,

AND BEHOLD KING SOLOMON

WITH THE CROWN WHEREWITH HIS MOTHER

CROWNED HIM IN THE DAY OF HIS ESPOUSALS,

AND IN THE DAY OF THE GLADNESS OF HIS HEART.

CHAPTER 4

BEHOLD, THOU ART FAIR, MY LOVE;

BEHOLD, THOU ART FAIR;

THOU HAST DOVES' EYES WITHIN THY LOCKS:

THY HAIR IS AS A FLOCK OF GOATS,

THAT APPEAR FROM MOUNT GILEAD.

2 THY TEETH ARE LIKE A FLOCK OF SHEEP

gednoſtegných /kdyż wycházegj z kupadla/
z nichž kaʒdá mjwá po dwém /a mezy nimiż
nenj żádné neplodné.

3 Gako prowázek z hedbáwj červeného,
dwakrát barweného, rtowé twogi° / a řeč
twá ozdobná : gako kus gablka zrnatého
gſau żidowiny twé mezy kadeři twými.

4 Hrdlo´ twé, geſt gako wěʒe Dawido-
wa, wyſtawená k chowánj zbroge/ w njż
na tiſýce pawéz wiſý / wſſe ſſtjtů muʒů
vdatných :

5 Oba twé prſy´ gako dwé telátek bli-
ʒencůw ſrnjch/genż ſe paſau w kwjtj.

6 Aʒby ˢzawjtal ten den/ a vtekliby ſtj-
nowé/ poodegdu k hoře mirrowé/ a pa-
hrbku kadidlowému .

7 Wſſecka gſy kráſná´ přjtelkyné má/ a
nenj na tobé poſſkwrny.

8 Semnau z Libánu , ó´Choti má, ſe-
mnau z Libánu půgdeš : a pohledjš s
´wrchu hory Amanah/s wrchu hory Se-
nyr, a Hermon / z peleſſj lwowých / a s
hor pardowých.

9 Gala ſy ſrdce mé, ſeſtro má Choti/ga-
la ſy ſrdce mé gednjm wzezřenjm očj ſwých/
a gedinau točenicý hrdla ſwého.

10 Gak °vtéſſené gſau miloſti twé, ſeſtro
má Choti! gak mnohem ᵖwʒácnégſſj gſau

THAT ARE EVEN SHORN, WHICH CAME UP FROM THE WASHING;

WHEREOF EVERY ONE BEAR TWINS, AND NONE IS BARREN AMONG THEM.

3 THY LIPS ARE LIKE A THREAD OF SCARLET,

AND THY SPEECH IS COMELY: THY TEMPLES

ARE LIKE A PIECE OF A POMEGRANATE WITHIN THY LOCKS.

4 THY NECK IS LIKE THE TOWER OF DAVID BUILDED

FOR AN ARMOURY, WHEREON THERE HANG

A THOUSAND BUCKLERS, ALL SHIELDS OF MIGHTY MEN.

5 THY TWO BREASTS ARE LIKE TWO YOUNG ROES

THAT ARE TWINS, WHICH FEED AMONG THE LILIES.

6 UNTIL THE DAY BREAK, AND THE SHADOWS FLEE AWAY,

I WILL GET ME TO THE MOUNTAIN OF MYRRH,

AND TO THE HILL OF FRANKINCENSE.

7 THOU ART ALL FAIR, MY LOVE; THERE IS NO SPOT IN THEE.

8 COME WITH ME FROM LEBANON, MY SPOUSE,

WITH ME FROM LEBANON: LOOK FROM THE TOP

OF AMANA, FROM THE TOP OF SHENIR AND HERMON,

FROM THE LIONS' DENS, FROM THE MOUNTAINS OF THE LEOPARDS.

9 THOU HAST RAVISHED MY HEART, MY SISTER, MY SPOUSE;

THOU HAST RAVISHED MY HEART WITH ONE OF THINE EYES,

WITH ONE CHAIN OF THY NECK.

10 HOW FAIR IS THY LOVE, MY SISTER, MY SPOUSE!

milofti twé neʒ wjno⁹ / a wůné maftj twých nadewffecky wonné wécyʳ.

11 Strdj tekau rtowé twogiˢ ó choti: med a mléko pod gaʒykem twým /a wůné raucha twého gako wůné Libánu.

12 Gako ʒahrada ʒamćenáᵗ gfy feftro má choti: gako wrchowifftěᵘ ʒamćené / a ftu-dnice ʒapećetenáᵂ:

13 ˣWyftřelkowé twogi gfau gako ʸʒa-hrada fftěpy ʒrnatých gablek wyfaʒená, s owocem roʒkoffiným /gahodek ˣcyprowých s nardem:

14 Nardu s ffaffránem / ᶻpruftworce s fkořicý / a s każdým ftromowjm kadidło wydáwagjcým: mirry aᵃaloes, y s wffeli-gakými ʒwláfftnjmi wécmi wonnými.

15 ◄O ty fám wrchowifftě ʒahradnj / ftudnice wod ʒiwých /a pramenowé tekaucý ʒ Libánuᵇ.

16 ᶜWég wětřjčku půlnočnj / a přiď wě-třjčku polednjᵈ / prowég ʒahradu mau /ať tekau wonné wécy gegj /a ať přigde miłý

HOW MUCH BETTER IS THY LOVE THAN WINE!

AND THE SMELL OF THINE OINTMENTS THAN ALL SPICES!

11 THY LIPS, O MY SPOUSE, DROP AS THE HONEYCOMB:

HONEY AND MILK ARE UNDER THY TONGUE;

AND THE SMELL OF THY GARMENTS IS LIKE THE SMELL OF LEBANON.

12 A GARDEN INCLOSED IS MY SISTER, MY SPOUSE;

A SPRING SHUT UP, A FOUNTAIN SEALED.

13 THY PLANTS ARE AN ORCHARD OF POMEGRANATES,

WITH PLEASANT FRUITS; CAMPHIRE, WITH SPIKENARD,

14 SPIKENARD AND SAFFRON; CALAMUS AND CINNAMON,

WITH ALL TREES OF FRANKINCENSE;

MYRRH AND ALOES, WITH ALL THE CHIEF SPICES:

15 A FOUNTAIN OF GARDENS, A WELL OF LIVING WATERS,

AND STREAMS FROM LEBANON.

16 AWAKE, O NORTH WIND;

AND COME, THOU SOUTH;

BLOW UPON MY GARDEN,

THAT THE SPICES THEREOF MAY FLOW OUT.

LET MY BELOVED COME INTO HIS GARDEN,

AND EAT HIS PLEASANT FRUITS.

můg do zahrady swé° / a gj rozkoſſné owo=
ce' ſwé°.

Kapitola   V.

Wſſelť ſem giž do zahrady ſwé°,
ſeſtro má, Choti: zbjrám mir=
ru ſwau⁶ y giné wonné wécy
ſwé: gjn plášť ſwůg, y med
ſwůg: pigi wjno ſwé, a mléko ſwé°: geſte
přátelé, pjte, a hogné ſe napjte mogi milj°.

2 ¶Spáwámé° nekdy, a wſſak ſrdce mé
bdj, nadto hlas milého mého tlukaucýho,
ſlýchám; ³Otewři mi 'ſeſtro má, přjtelky=
né má, holubičko má, ³wprjmá má: nebo
hlawa má plná geſt roſy⁶ / a kadeře mé,
krupégj nočních.

3 Odpowéděla ſem; Swlékla ſem ſukni
ſwau, kterakž gi zaſe obleku? vmyla ſem
nohy ſwé, což ge mám zaſe zmazati'?

CHAPTER 5

I AM COME INTO MY GARDEN, MY SISTER, MY SPOUSE:

I HAVE GATHERED MY MYRRH WITH MY SPICE;

I HAVE EATEN MY HONEYCOMB WITH MY HONEY;

I HAVE DRUNK MY WINE WITH MY MILK: EAT, O FRIENDS;

DRINK, YEA, DRINK ABUNDANTLY, O BELOVED.

2 I SLEEP, BUT MY HEART WAKETH: IT IS THE VOICE

OF MY BELOVED THAT KNOCKETH, SAYING,

OPEN TO ME, MY SISTER, MY LOVE, MY DOVE, MY UNDEFILED:

FOR MY HEAD IS FILLED WITH DEW, AND MY LOCKS

WITH THE DROPS OF THE NIGHT.

3 I HAVE PUT OFF MY COAT; HOW SHALL I PUT IT ON?

I HAVE WASHED MY FEET;

HOW SHALL I DEFILE THEM?

4 Milý můg sáhl rukau swau ˡſkrze dwéře / a ˡwnitřnoſti mé ᵐpohnuly ſe ⁿwemné

5 Ja wſtala ſem, abych otewřela milému ſwému: a ay z rukau mých kapala mirra/ y z prſtů mých, a to mirra tekutá/ gakž ſem ſáhla k rukowétem° záwory:

6 Otewřelať ſem byla milému ſwému: ale milý můg giž byl vſſel, a pominul: duſſe má téměř byla wyſſla zemne, když on promluwil:ˡhledalaſem ho/ale nenaſſla ſé ho: wolala ſem ho/ ale neozwal ſe miᵖ.

7 Nalezſſeˢ mne ſtrážnjʳ, kteřjž chodj po méſté, zbili mne/ranili mne:wzali nadto y rauchu°mau ſeinne,ſtrážnj zdj méſtſkých

8 ˡZawazugi wás přjſahau, dcery Geruzalémſké/ geſtližebyſſte naſſly milého mého, co gemu powjte: A to/že ſem nemocna welikau miloſtjᵗ.

9* ¶Což má milý twůg mimo giné milé/ óneykráſněgſſj zžen:᷎co má milý twůg nad giné milé/že nás tak přjſahau zawazugeš:

10 ˡ¶Milý můg geſt ⁿbjlý a čerweny / ⁿznamenitéſſj nežli deſet tiſýců᷎v giných.

11 Hlawa geho gako ryzý zlatoʳ / wlaſy geho kadeřawéⁿ,černé gako hawran.

12 Očiᵇgeho gako holubic,nad ſtokywod/ gako w mléce vmyté, ⁿſtogjcý w ſluſſnoſti

13 Ljceᵇgeho gako záhonky wonnými wé

120

4 MY BELOVED PUT IN HIS HAND BY THE HOLE OF THE DOOR,

AND MY BOWELS WERE MOVED FOR HIM.

5 I ROSE UP TO OPEN TO MY BELOVED; AND MY HANDS

DROPPED WITH MYRRH, AND MY FINGERS

WITH SWEET SMELLING MYRRH, UPON THE HANDLES OF THE LOCK.

6 I OPENED TO MY BELOVED; BUT MY BELOVED HAD WITHDRAWN
HIMSELF,
AND WAS GONE; MY SOUL FAILED WHEN HE SPAKE;

I SOUGHT HIM, BUT I COULD NOT FIND HIM;

I CALLED HIM, BUT HE GAVE ME NO ANSWER.

7 THE WATCHMEN THAT WENT ABOUT THE CITY FOUND ME,

THEY SMOTE ME, THEY WOUNDED ME;

THE KEEPERS OF THE WALLS TOOK AWAY MY VEIL FROM ME.

8 I CHARGE YOU, O DAUGHTERS OF JERUSALEM, IF YE FIND MY
BELOVED,
THAT YE TELL HIM, THAT I AM SICK OF LOVE.

9 WHAT IS THY BELOVED MORE THAN ANOTHER BELOVED,

O THOU FAIREST AMONG WOMEN? WHAT IS THY BELOVED

MORE THAN ANOTHER BELOVED, THAT THOU DOST SO CHARGE US?

10 MY BELOVED IS WHITE AND RUDDY, THE CHIEFEST AMONG TEN
THOUSAND.
11 HIS HEAD IS AS THE MOST FINE GOLD, HIS LOCKS ARE BUSHY,

AND BLACK AS A RAVEN.

12 HIS EYES ARE AS THE EYES OF DOVES BY THE RIVERS OF WATERS,

WASHED WITH MILK, AND FITLY SET.

cmi *wyſazené* / gako ᵉkwětowé wonných wěcý: rtowé geho gako lilium, prýſſtýcý ₃ ſebe **mirru tekutau.**

₁₄ Ruce geho **kráſné,** gako ᵇprſtenowé zlatj, wyſazenj kamenjm drahým / gako ᶜHyacynktem: ᶠbřicho geho gako ſtkwě‑ ⸲oſt ſlonowé koſti Zaſſjry obloʒené.

₁₅ Hnátowé ᵍgeho gako ſlaupowé mra‑ morowj, na podſtawcých ʒlata neýčiſt‑ ſſjho ʒaloʒenj: ʰobljceg geho gako Libán, giné ᶦprewyſſugjcý gako Cedrowé.

₁₆ Vſtaᶠ geho ᶦpřeſladká, a wſſecken geſt ·přeʒádoſtiwý / takowýť geſt milý můg / takowý geſt prawjm přjtel můg, ō dcery Geruʒalémſké.

₁₇ ¶Kamʒe pak odſſel milý twůg, ō ney‑ kráſnégſſj ʒʒen? kam ſe obrátil milý twůg / a hledati ho budeme s tebau?

Kapitola VI.

ᶠMilý můg sſtaupil doʒahrady⸴ ſwé / k ʒáhonkům wěcý won‑ ných / aby páſl w ᵇʒahradách / a aby zbjral lilium.

₂ *Gáᶦ gſem milého mého / a milý můg, geſt můg / kterýʒ paſe meʒy lilium.

₃ ‡¶Kráſná gſy přjtelkyně má, gako Terſaᶜ: pěkná, gako Geruʒalém: hroʒná

122

13 HIS CHEEKS ARE AS A BED OF SPICES, AS SWEET FLOWERS:

HIS LIPS LIKE LILIES, DROPPING SWEET SMELLING MYRRH.

14 HIS HANDS ARE AS GOLD RINGS SET WITH THE BERYL:

HIS BELLY IS AS BRIGHT IVORY

OVERLAID WITH SAPPHIRES.

15 HIS LEGS ARE AS PILLARS OF MARBLE,

SET UPON SOCKETS OF FINE GOLD:

HIS COUNTENANCE IS AS LEBANON, EXCELLENT AS THE CEDARS.

16 HIS MOUTH IS MOST SWEET:

YEA, HE IS ALTOGETHER LOVELY.

THIS IS MY BELOVED, AND THIS IS MY FRIEND,

O DAUGHTERS OF JERUSALEM.

17 WHITHER IS THY BELOVED GONE, O THOU FAIREST

AMONG WOMEN? WHITHER IS THY BELOVED TURNED ASIDE?

THAT WE MAY SEEK HIM WITH THEE.

CHAPTER 6

MY BELOVED IS GONE DOWN INTO HIS GARDEN,

TO THE BEDS OF SPICES, TO FEED IN THE GARDENS,

AND TO GATHER LILIES.

2 I AM MY BELOVED'S, AND MY BELOVED IS MINE:

HE FEEDETH AMONG THE LILIES.

3 THOU ART BEAUTIFUL, O MY LOVE, AS TIRZAH,

ᵇgako wogſko s praporcy.

4 ᶜOdwrať oči ſwé od patřenj na mne /
ᶠneb ony mne poſylugjˢ:ᵗwłaſy twé gſau ga
ko ſtáda koz/kteréž wjdati na hoře Galád.

5 ˣZubowé twogi gſau podobnj ſtádu
owcý, když wycházegj z kupadla/z nichž
každá mjwá po dwém/a mezy nimiž nenj
žádné neplodné.

6 ᶻGako kus gablka zrnatého gſau žido-
winy twé, mezy kadeři twými.

7 Ačkoli geſt ſſedeſáte králowen/ a oſm-
deſáte ženinᵗ/ a mladic bez počtuʰ/

8 Gediná geſt wſſak má holubice/ má
ⁱvpřjmá: gedinká při matce ſwé/ᵏnepoſk-
wrněná při ſwé rodićceˡ: ſpatřiwſſe gi takowau giné dceryᵐ/blahoſlawily gi/ano y
králowny, a ženiny/y chwálily gi, řkauce;

9 ᶻKteráᵖ geſt to ⁿkterauž widěti gako
dennicy/ kráſná gako měſýc/ čiſtá gako
ſlunce/hrozná gako wogſko s praporcy?

10ᵖᶻDo ᵖzahrady wyprawenéᵍ ſtaupila
ſem/abych ſpatřilaʳ owoce při vdolj: abych
widěla, kweteli winný kmen/ a pučjli ſe

124

COMELY AS JERUSALEM, TERRIBLE AS AN ARMY WITH BANNERS.

4 TURN AWAY THINE EYES FROM ME, FOR THEY HAVE OVERCOME
ME:

THY HAIR IS AS A FLOCK OF GOATS THAT APPEAR FROM GILEAD.

5 THY TEETH ARE AS A FLOCK OF SHEEP WHICH GO UP

FROM THE WASHING, WHEREOF EVERY ONE BEARETH TWINS,

AND THERE IS NOT ONE BARREN AMONG THEM.

6 AS A PIECE OF A POMEGRANATE

ARE THY TEMPLES WITHIN THY LOCKS.

7 THERE ARE THREESCORE QUEENS, AND FOURSCORE CONCUBINES,

AND VIRGINS WITHOUT NUMBER.

8 MY DOVE, MY UNDEFILED IS BUT ONE;

SHE IS THE ONLY ONE OF HER MOTHER, SHE IS THE CHOICE ONE OF
HER

THAT BARE HER. THE DAUGHTERS SAW HER, AND BLESSED HER;

YEA, THE QUEENS AND THE CONCUBINES, AND THEY PRAISED HER.

9 WHO IS SHE THAT LOOKETH FORTH AS THE MORNING,

FAIR AS THE MOON, CLEAR AS THE SUN,

AND TERRIBLE AS AN ARMY WITH BANNERS?

gabloně zrnaté:

11 Nezwěděla sem/a ˢžádoſt má ponukla mne na wůz ᵗpřednějſſjch z lidu mého.

12 ᵛNawrať ſe, nawrať ó Sulamitſká" / nawrať ſe, nawrať, ať naté patřjme ʷ. ᶻCo vzřjte na Sulamitſké? Gako záſtup wo᛫ genſký ˣ.

Kapitola VII.

ᵃAk ſau kráſné nohy twé" w tře wjcých, dcero knjžecý⁶ ! oko᛫ lek bedr twých" gako zápony, djlo rukau wýborného řemeſl njka.

2 Pupek twůg gako koſſljk okrauhlý, nebezᵈnápoge : břicho twé gako ſtoh pſſe᛫ nice obroſtlý kwjtjm".

3 ᶻOba twé prſy gako dwé telátek bli᛫ žencůw ſrnjch.

126

10 I WENT DOWN INTO THE GARDEN OF NUTS

TO SEE THE FRUITS OF THE VALLEY,

AND TO SEE WHETHER THE VINE FLOURISHED,

AND THE POMEGRANATES BUDDED.

11 OR EVER I WAS AWARE, MY SOUL MADE ME

LIKE THE CHARIOTS OF AMMINADIB.

12 RETURN, RETURN, O SHULAMITE; RETURN, RETURN,

THAT WE MAY LOOK UPON THEE.

WHAT WILL YE SEE IN THE SHULAMITE?

AS IT WERE THE COMPANY OF TWO ARMIES.

CHAPTER 7

HOW BEAUTIFUL ARE THY FEET WITH SHOES,

O PRINCE'S DAUGHTER! THE JOINTS OF THY THIGHS ARE LIKE
JEWELS.
THE WORK OF THE HANDS OF A CUNNING WORKMAN.

2 THY NAVEL IS LIKE A ROUND GOBLET,

WHICH WANTETH NOT LIQUOR: THY BELLY

IS LIKE AN HEAP OF WHEAT SET ABOUT WITH LILIES.

3 THY TWO BREASTS ARE LIKE TWO YOUNG ROES THAT ARE TWINS.

4 *Hrdlo twé gako wěže z koſtj ſlonowých: oči twé gako rybnjcyſ w Ezebon / podlé ᵃbrány Batrabbim: nos twůg gako wěže Libánſkáᵇ patřjcý k Damaſſku.

5 Hlawa twá na tobě gako Karmelᶜ/a ᵈwlaſy hlawy twé gſau kráſné gako ſſarlat: tak že král přiwázánby byl na pawlačjch twýchˡ.

6 Gak gſy ty kráſná/ a gak vtěſſená, ō miloſti ᵐpřerozkoſſná!

7 Tato ⁿpoſtawa twá podobna geſt palméᵒ/a prſy ᵖtwé broznům.

8 ᴵᵗRekla semᵖ; Wſtaupjm na palmu/ a doſáhnu wrchůw gegjch: nechažť mi te dy gſau prſy twé gako broznowé winného kmene/a wůně chřjpj twých gako gablek wonných :

9 Vſta twá gako wjno wýborné, ᵗmně milá pro vpřjmoſt / půſobjcý, aby y těch genž ſpj. rtowé mluwiliʳ.

10ᵗ ᴵGá ſem milého ſwého/a kemně geſt žádoſt ˢgeho.

128

4 THY NECK IS AS A TOWER OF IVORY; THINE EYES

LIKE THE FISHPOOLS IN HESHBON, BY THE GATE OF BATHRABBIM:

THY NOSE IS AS THE TOWER OF LEBANON

WHICH LOOKETH TOWARD DAMASCUS.

5 THINE HEAD UPON THEE IS LIKE CARMEL,

AND THE HAIR OF THINE HEAD LIKE PURPLE;

THE KING IS HELD IN THE GALLERIES.

6 HOW FAIR AND HOW PLEASANT ART THOU, O LOVE, FOR
                                                     DELIGHTS!
7 THIS THY STATURE IS LIKE TO A PALM TREE,

AND THY BREASTS TO CLUSTERS OF GRAPES.

8 I SAID, I WILL GO UP TO THE PALM TREE,

I WILL TAKE HOLD OF THE BOUGHS THEREOF:

NOW ALSO THY BREASTS SHALL BE AS CLUSTERS OF THE VINE,

AND THE SMELL OF THY NOSE LIKE APPLES;

9 AND THE ROOF OF THY MOUTH LIKE THE BEST WINE FOR MY
                                                   BELOVED,
THAT GOETH DOWN SWEETLY,

CAUSING THE LIPS OF THOSE THAT ARE ASLEEP TO SPEAK.

10 I AM MY BELOVED'S, AND HIS DESIRE IS TOWARD ME.

11 ᵗPoď milý můg : wygděme na pole/ a přenocůgne ᵘwe wſech:

12 Ráno wſtanauce, půgdeme ᵂᵏ winicým/pohledjme, kweteli winný kmen/giżli ſe ˣvkázal začátek hroznů/kwetauli gablka zrnatá : a tuť dám tobé miloſti ſwéʸ.

13 ᶻPékná gablčka wydala wůniᶻ ſwau/ a přі dweřjch naſſich gſau wſſecky rozkoſſeᵃ, ᵇnowé y ſtaréᶜ: to wſſe milý můg, zachowala ſem tobé.

Kapitola VIII.

ᵃBy byl gako bratr můg, poźjwagjcý prſý matky mé/abych té naleznuc wné, poljbila / a nebyla zahanbenaᵇ:

2 Wedlabych té/a vwedla do domu matky ſwéᵗ: a tuby mne wyvčowal : agáť bych dala pjti wjna ᵈſtrogeného/a mſtu z gablek zrnatýchᵈ.

3 ᵉLewice geho geſt pod hlawau mau/ a prawicý ſwau obgjmá mne.

4 ᵗᵗPřjſahau wás zawazugi dcery Geru

11 COME, MY BELOVED, LET US GO FORTH INTO THE FIELD;

LET US LODGE IN THE VILLAGES.

12 LET US GET UP EARLY TO THE VINEYARDS; LET US SEE

IF THE VINE FLOURISH, WHETHER THE TENDER GRAPE APPEAR,

AND THE POMEGRANATES BUD FORTH: THERE WILL I GIVE THEE MY
LOVES.

13 THE MANDRAKES GIVE A SMELL, AND AT OUR GATES

ARE ALL MANNER OF PLEASANT FRUITS,

NEW AND OLD, WHICH I HAVE LAID UP FOR THEE, O MY BELOVED.

CHAPTER 8

O THAT THOU WERT AS MY BROTHER,

THAT SUCKED THE BREASTS OF MY MOTHER!

WHEN I SHOULD FIND THEE WITHOUT,

I WOULD KISS THEE; YEA, I SHOULD NOT BE DESPISED.

2 I WOULD LEAD THEE, AND BRING THEE INTO MY MOTHER'S HOUSE,

WHO WOULD INSTRUCT ME: I WOULD CAUSE THEE

TO DRINK OF SPICED WINE OF THE JUICE OF MY POMEGRANATE.

3 HIS LEFT HAND SHOULD BE UNDER MY HEAD,

AND HIS RIGHT HAND SHOULD EMBRACE ME.

4 I CHARGE YOU, O DAUGHTERS OF JERUSALEM,

zalémſké: ʻabyſſte nebudiły a newyrážeły zeſna ſmilého mého/ dokudžby ſam nechtěl.

5 Která geſt to genž wſtupugeˢ z pau ſtě, zpolehſſi na milého ſwého? Pod ga blonj wzbudiła ſem tě⁴/ tuť tebe počała matka twá /tuť tebe počała rodička twá'.

6 Položiž mne tedy gako pečet na ſrdce ſwéᶠ /a gako pečetnj prſten na ruku ſwau: nebo ſylné geſt gako ſmrt miłowánj': twr dá gako ᵐhrob horliwoſt : vhlj gegj, vhlj řeřawé/ a gako plamen ⁿneyprudſſj:

7 Ani wody mnohé nemohłyby vhaſyti tohoto miłowánj/ aniž ho řeky zatopj: kdyby ʻněkdo dáti chtěł wſſecken ſtatek do mu ſwého za takowau miłoſt / ᴾ ſewſſjm tjm pohrdnut by był.

8 Seſtruᵠ mámeʳ maličkauˢ / kteráž ge ſtě nemá prſý: co včinjmeᵗ 8 ſeſtrau ſwau, w den w kterýž bude řeč onjᵘ?

9 ↑ ¶Geſtliže geſt gako zed ʷ /wzděláme nanj palác ſtřjbrnýˣ: pakli geſt dweřmiʸ/

THAT YE STIR NOT UP, NOR AWAKE MY LOVE, UNTIL HE PLEASE.

5 WHO IS THIS THAT COMETH UP FROM THE WILDERNESS,

LEANING UPON HER BELOVED? I RAISED THEE UP

UNDER THE APPLE TREE: THERE THY MOTHER BROUGHT THEE
FORTH:
THERE SHE BROUGHT THEE FORTH THAT BARE THEE.

6 SET ME AS A SEAL UPON THINE HEART,

AS A SEAL UPON THINE ARM: FOR LOVE IS STRONG AS DEATH;

JEALOUSY IS CRUEL AS THE GRAVE: THE COALS THEREOF

ARE COALS OF FIRE, WHICH HATH A MOST VEHEMENT FLAME.

7 MANY WATERS CANNOT QUENCH LOVE,

NEITHER CAN THE FLOODS DROWN IT: IF A MAN WOULD GIVE

ALL THE SUBSTANCE OF HIS HOUSE FOR LOVE,

IT WOULD UTTERLY BE CONTEMNED.

8 WE HAVE A LITTLE SISTER, AND SHE HATH NO BREASTS:

WHAT SHALL WE DO FOR OUR SISTER IN THE DAY

WHEN SHE SHALL BE SPOKEN FOR?

9 IF SHE BE A WALL, WE WILL BUILD UPON HER A PALACE OF
SILVER:
AND IF SHE BE A DOOR

133

obložjme ge dckami cedrowými.

10 ¶ Gá gſem zed'/a prſy mé gſau gako
wěže: takž ſem y hned byla před oćima geho, gakožto ta genž nacházý pokog[a].

11 ¶ Winicy měl Sſalomaun w Bal-
hamon/ kteraužto pronagal ſtrážným:
tak aby gedenkaždý přináſſel za owoce
gegj, tiſýc ſtřjbrných:

12 Ale winice má, kterauž mám, přede-
mnau geſt': mĕgž ſobě těch tiſýc ſtřjbrných,
ó Sſalomaune/ a dwě ſtě ti kteřjž oſtřjha-
gj owoce gegjho.

13 O ty kteráž bydljš w zahradách[c]/ přátelé rádi pozorugj hlaſu twého / ohlá-
ſůgž mi ſe.

14 ¶ Poſpěš milý můg[g]/ a připodobni ſe
k ſrně, neb mladému gelenu/ na horách
wonných wěcý[h].

WE WILL INCLOSE HER WITH BOARDS OF CEDAR.

10 I AM A WALL, AND MY BREASTS LIKE TOWERS:

THEN WAS I IN HIS EYES AS ONE THAT FOUND FAVOUR.

11 SOLOMON HAD A VINEYARD AT BAALHAMON;

HE LET OUT THE VINEYARD UNTO KEEPERS;

EVERY ONE FOR THE FRUIT THEREOF

WAS TO BRING A THOUSAND PIECES OF SILVER.

12 MY VINEYARD, WHICH IS MINE, IS BEFORE ME:

THOU, O SOLOMON, MUST HAVE A THOUSAND,

AND THOSE THAT KEEP THE FRUIT THEREOF TWO HUNDRED.

13 THOU THAT DWELLEST IN THE GARDENS,

THE COMPANIONS HEARKEN TO THY VOICE: CAUSE ME TO HEAR IT.

14 MAKE HASTE, MY BELOVED,

AND BE THOU LIKE TO A ROE

OR TO A YOUNG HART UPON THE MOUNTAINS OF SPICES.

SYMBOLVM SIMONIS LOMNICENI à BVDCZE.

Syncere & Liberè.

Vpřjmně čiň a Swobodně/
Budeſſ ctěn ſſanowán hodně.

ŠIMON LOMNICKÝ z BUDČE (1552-1623) was a scholarly retainer of the aristocratic house of Rosenberg. A Catholic himself, he published two books of hymns, a verse epic on the life of the biblical Joseph, verse drama in the medieval style, and occasional poetry: the following heraldic verses were written in honour of his patron. Lomnický lived to see the defeat of the Czech Protestant armies by the forces of King Ferdinand: the poet was himself compromised with the rebel movement, and after its collapse he fell from favour and died in obscure poverty.

A vivid literary document of the time were the verses, published anonymously, on the fate of the rebel leaders in 1621. The poem Exekuce was attributed to Lomnicky by his contemporary. P. Skála ze Zhoře, then in exile: the attribution was accepted without question until recent times, when research exposed its improbability.

137

Wylém z Rožmbergka/ a na Cžeškém Krumlowě/ Pán a wládař Domu Rožmberského/ Rytýř Towaryšstwa Zlatého Rauna 2c. Neywyšší Purgkhrabě Králowstwj Cžeského.

Wším Zahrádku vtěšenau/
Cžerným Lesem ohrazenau
W té Zahrádce krasná Růže/
W Zymě/w Letě kwěsti může.
K obw ašenh té Růžičko/
Plyne woda pod nij wjdyčky.

K tomu w té Zahrádce mareš
Při té Ruži Rau ao Zlaté.
Stogj v nij dwa Nedwěd̄/
Pilné gij c̄straha: hebu.
Sam va Huh ke en ſiwě chwále
Ostrhanj té Ruže Rzlě.

ERB ROŽMBERSKÝ

Šimon
Lomnický
z Budče
(1590)

Vím zahrádku utěšenou,
černým lesem ohrazenou,
    v té zahrádce krásná růže
    v zimě v létě kvísti může

K ovlažení té růžičky
plyne voda pod ní vždycky,
    k tomu v té zahrádce máte
    při té růži rouno zlaté.

Stojí u ni dva medvědi,
pilně ji ostříhat hledí,
    sám Pán Bůh k své cti a chvále
    ostříhejž té růže dále.

THE ROSENBERG COAT
OF ARMS

Translated
by Iris
Sindelar

I know a delightful garden,
Bounded by a gloomy forest;
    There a lovely rose is blooming,
    All the year its beauty showing.

Close beneath that rose so tender
Water flows to guard its growing,
    And beside it, in that garden,
    You will find a fleece of gold.

Near the rose two bears are standing,
Carefully they watch to guard it;
    God himself, for praise and honor,
    Will protect that rose forever.

Regſtřjk a Poznamenánj/
Kteřj gſau a gak treſtáni/
Pro to ſwé Rebellowánj/
Měſſťané také y Páni.

Stjnáni a Mečem treſtáni tito:

1. Joachym Ondřeg/ Hrabě Sſljk/
   k tomu Ruka vťatá.
2. Wáclaw Budowec.
3. Kryſtoff Harant.
4. Kaſſpar Kapljř.
5. Prokop Dwořecký.
6. Frydrych z Bílé.
7. Gindřich Otta.
8. Wylém Konecchlumſký.
9. Bohuſlaw z Michalowic/
   k tomu Ruka vťata.
10. Diwiſſ Cžernin. ✠
11. Walentin Kochan.
12. Tobiáſſ Šteffek.

13. Kry⸗

EXEKUCE

Každý podlé provinění
svou pokutu nesl,
nebyl také bez trápení,
kdož jazykem klesl.
    A tak, jakož práva svědčí,
    kdo měl provinění větší,
    měl pokutu těžši.

140

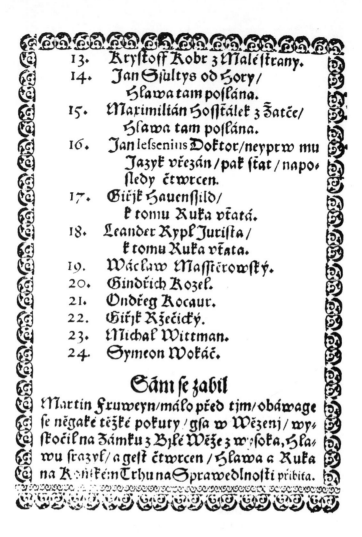

So every one was punished
according to his wrong:
nor were they spared the torment
whose fault lay in their tongue.
   And as the law requires
   according to his conduct
   each suffered for his crimes.

Translated
by Alfred
French

141

Někteří vypovědéni
jsou z země na věčnost
a jiní ještě v vězení
čekají na milost,
opět vymrskáni jiní,
rebelové jsou tím vinni,
co se koli činí.

Ó přežalostné divadlo,
mnozí se užásli
a nejedněm srdce chřadlo,
až se hrůzou třásli,
nebo není pamětníka
aby nastala tolika
tak žalost veliká.

Dvanácte hlav vystrčeno
na mostě na bráně,
aby bylo rozhlášeno
v každé světa straně,
kdo jsou byli rebelové,
nešťastní direktorové,
zlého původové.

Čtvrti na rozcestí dány
po každé silnici,
ano ruce zutínány
ty prsty mající,
jenž falešně přisahaly
a nahoru se zdvíhaly,
věrnost slibovaly.

Tolik osob zahynulo
dosti v malé chvíli
a jeden den jich minulo,
přišli k svému cíli.
Bože, pro sebe samého
takového pádu zlého
uchovej každého.

Some driven out for ever
in exile from their race;
while others lie in prison
in hope of royal grace.
      And for all that grief and pain,
      for the beatings and the whippings,
      the Rebels are to blame.

So many were confounded
before that dreadful sight:
and many a spirit fainted
in shock and horrid fright.
      Such depths of agony
      had never yet been witnessed
      in human memory.

Twelve heads upon the Bridge tower
were set before men's eyes,
that all the world should witness,
and all should recognise
      who sinned against the King,
      the ill-fated Directors,
      that caused the suffering.

At the crossroads of the city
the quartered bodies lay:
and others suffered despite,
whose hands were chopped away
      to purge their treachery—
      the fingers raised in falsehood
      that pledged their loyalty.

Within so brief an hour
so many lives were done:
their span on earth was over
their day of life was run.
      From such a dreadful fall
      may Jesus save us all!
      Dear Lord, preserve us all!

143

Začjná se Pjseň o Wykonánj Weypo-
wědi a Ortele hrozného nad Rebelly Geho
Milosti Cýsařské/Králi a Pánu naššemu nep-
milostiwěaššimu Ferdynandowi
Druhému/2c.

¶ Gako: Ach, ach, auwech na móhoře/
kam se mám podýti/2c.

Lý začátek, zlé skončenj wždy-
Ten srozumj že klam nenj/kdo

cky téměř mjwá.
Pjseň přezpjwá: Ro/ Zle začali Kal-

winowé/ zle dokonali Stawowé/

wšickni Rebelľowé.

A ij   ¶ Ano

$\mathcal{M}$IKULÁŠ DAČICKÝ z HESLOVA (1555-1626) has left, besides a book of memoirs, a collection of verse written in a critical, realistic, style, and directed to the social conditions of his time. Like Lomnický, he lived to see the collapse of the Czech Protestant movement at the battle of the White Mountain in 1620, and the occupation of Bohemia by alien masters: patriotism, and the call to resistence, became basic themes of his later verse. The following poem stands in the literary record at the head of a long sequence of similar works by many poets on the denunciation of Bohemia's overlords, and the hope of eventual freedom. In his appeal to the distant past to justify the claim to Czech independence Dačický seems to be anticipating poetry of the Czech Revival of 200 years later.

145

Ó BOHEMIA

Mikuláš
Dačický
z Heslova

Není to v světě nic divného,
že vlast táhne k sobě svého;
Česká země hladovitého
živí i nepřítele mnohého.
Nemá odměny od žádného,
trpí od cizích mnoho zlého.
Ó, Bože, chraniž národu českého!

Předešle a za pohanstva
byla země Česká pusta,
zůstávaje tak od dávna
lidského rozumu prázdna.
Když pak z osudu božského
od národu slovanského
skrze Čecha osazena,
ve všem dobrém rozmnožena,
tu hned národové jiní,
závistiví, nepřízniví,
oč prvé nikda nestáli,
nestarali, nevzdělali,
zosobit usilovali
a do Čech se velmi drali,
chtíce to Čechuom vydříti,
z cizí práce rozkoš jmíti
a svou vůli provoditi,
o vše všudy připraviti,
o čež usilují až posavad,
aby ledakdos v Čechách vlád,
nemůže-li, aby okrad.

146

O BOHEMIA

A common instinct beckons men
towards their native land;
Bohemia's soil attracts her foes,
that swarming, hungry band.
And profiting from no man's hand
she suffers sore that alien brand.
God save our native land!

Bohemia was bare of men
in distant pagan days;
had never known since time began,
the touch of human ways.
And when, that God's will should be done,
the Slavic people came,
and Czech, our founder, filled the land,
it multiplied in fame.
Then other nations, filled with spite,
turned evil, envious eyes
on what till now they never sought
nor strove to civilise.
They swarmed into Bohemia
to seize our native soil,
to grind the Czechs to slavery
and live from others' toil;
to impose their will upon the land,
to rob, to plunder her;
and steadfastly they seek this end
to dominate Bohemia,
or else to ravish her.

Translated
by A.
French

147

Ó, kde jsou starých Čechuov ruce
na takové cizozemce.
Nynější se jen dívají,
mnozí i napomáhají,
tak k záhubě pospíchají.
K čemu přijdou, to poznají.

Jmějž se dobře, milý Čechu,
nelez dále do posměchu.
Každý do tvé vlasti běží,
tak zůstáváš jen v loupeži.
Ochraňujž sám Pán Buoh tebe
a pomoz z země do nebe.

Where now the ancient Czechs that smote   O Bohemia
the stranger at the gate?
For men today stand by and watch,
or some collaborate;
they rush towards their doom, nor yet
they realise their fate.

O fare thee well, good Czech! Stoop not
to worse humiliation!
the target of each alien band,
the prey of every nation.
God shield you, that you yet may rise,
from earth unto the skies!

150

he hundred and fifty years which followed the disaster at the White Mountain have generally been regarded as a dark age of Czech cultural life. The dominion of foreigners, the loss of all freedom of expression, the physical impoverishment of the land, the rigidly administered conditions of education and publication, and the disappearance of an educated audience for Czech literary products—all these conditions tended towards a complete break-down of national culture. On the other hand the threat to the existence of the Czechs as a people drew the attention of its members to the links which bound them together. It was their history, their traditions, above all their language, which marked them off as a group from their Germanic neighbours. Through this dangerous period the Czechs preserved their oral and folk traditions because, without them there was no solidarity left for the national group. Persecution and humiliation acted to revive the appeal of Czech folk poetry which becomes of great interest and importance for future writers.

The complete success of the Counter-reformation in Bohemia was partly due to the ruthless efficiency with which religious re-forms were enforced by state authority. But the struggle for men's allegiance was carried on in more positive ways. Hymns in the Czech language had been one way in which the Hussites had in-volved the common folk in the ceremonial of the church, and from the early days of the seventeenth century Catholic hymns were composed, sung and published in Czech. From these begin-nings there sprang a whole crop of lyric verse. At first it was purely liturgical, then it spread from the religious into the secular sphere, excelling the lyric harvest of the preceding century. Characteristic of this new poetry are the ecstatic visions of the transcendent universe viewed in and through the homely environment of this world. As the new skyline of rebuilt Prague with its false perspec-tives and soaring spires was designed to draw the eye of the viewer from earth to heaven, so too the sublime lyrics of Czech baroque, trembling between horror and exaltation, touched new horizons in art, and had a permanent, though long unacknowledged, effect on the development of Czech poetry.

151

POHRZENÍ POMÍJEJÍCÍHO SVĚTA

Adam
Václav
Michna z
Otradovic
(1661)

Co pomáhá světská sláva,
an pomíjí jako tráva?
   Dým v povětří větrem hyne,
   život náš dnes, zejtra mine.

Co trůn pánuv, berla králův,
co koruny potentátův?
   Všecko někdy vezme konec,
   smrt poslední chce mít tanec.

Co spomáhá krásným býti,
třebas tvář andělskou míti?
   Nejpěknější sprchá růže,
   v hrobě hnije tělo, kůže.

Měj i oči křišťálový,
měj i pysky korálový,
   bud' vlas žlutý víc než zlato,
   v brzkém čase bude bláto.

Měj zlatohlav neb hedbáví
a co koli oči vábí:
   zlato země jest červená,
   marná jest u lidí cena.

152

DISDAIN FOR THIS TRANSITORY WORLD

What avail is worldly glory?
Flesh like grass is transitory.
   Smoke we are, by rough winds carried,
   Here today, tomorrow buried.

What are royal throne and power,
Princely castle, knightly tower?
   All must come to dust and ashes:
   Death's last dance will end all passion.

What avail are youth and vigour,
Angel's face or fairest figure?
   E'en the rose must wilt and wither,
   Grave rots bone and skin together.

Be your eyes of crystal lightness,
Be your lips of coral brightness,
   Be your hair like red gold burning:
   Soon to clay it will be turning.

Rustling silk or golden treasure,
All which to the eye gives pleasure:
   Gold is sand, like sand you spend it;
   Vain the price that humans lend it.

Translated
by E. Osers

Co jest roucho šarlatové?
krev jest, lejno hlemejžd'ové,
   pejše musí sloužit moře,
   bude někdy těžké hoře.

Co choditi v aksamitě,
ošat'te se jak umíte,
   pošlo z červíčkův prediva,
   nač se světa pejcha dívá?

Co červ z sebe vyhazuje
velice člověk šacuje,
   v tom se sadí a nadýmá,
   své kochání, rozkoš mívá.

Měj se dobře marný světe,
kratičký dým, jarní květe,
   nedám se tobě mámiti,
   volím věčnou rozkoš míti.

Čiň jak tě tvá vede libost,
já nestojím o tvou milost,
   vzdychám, dychtím po věčnosti,
   časně sahám k pobožnosti.

What are crimson robe and ermine?
Merely blood and slime and vermin.
   Pride and riches will be humbled,
   Greatness mercilessly tumbled.

Ye who walk in velvet breeches:
Poverty the Master teaches!
   Silk is but the worm's extrusion,
   Worldly pride is but illusion.

What the silkworm has excreted,
Worthless, horrible and fetid,
   Man counts precious and entrancing:
   Silk he wears for feast and dancing.

So adieu, world of the senses,
Tempting me with vain pretences,
   Brief as smoke and flower vernal:
   I elect the joys eternal.

How the world behaves I care not,
In its vanity I share not:
   I am eager for salvation,
   Turn to pious meditation.

VERŠE O NEBESKÉM PALÁCI

Bedřich
Bridel
(1658)

Ach, ten nebeský palác
   jest jako ňáké lešení,
krásné dílo, modrý plac,
   jest libých hlasův slyšení.

Sedm hvězd, jenž tam hrají,
   jako sedmerého hlasu,
Bohu pěkně zpívají,
   jeho chválí vždycky krásu.

Slunce jest jedna struna,
   ozdoba jeho papršlek,
jakožto strun koruna,
   v níž osvěcuje okršlek.

Chceš li pak strun míti víc,
   buď malé nebo veliké,
vem sobě spolu měsíc
   i jiné hvězdy všeliké.

Když na ty housle hrají,
   na harfy nebo na loutny,
zdá se mi, že jsem v ráji,
   nedbám ani na koruny.

Láska muziku řídí,
   sama struny natahuje,
chtě vzbudit všechny lidi,
   sama zpívá i štymuje.

Poslyš, pěkně jak zpívá,
   již začíná, nastav uši,
všechna žádosti chtivá,
   chtěje pohnouti tvou duší.

POEM ON THE CELESTIAL PALACE

O, that celestial palace
Is like, like a latticed trellis,
Lovely scaffolding, blue place,
Full of the soft voices of space.

Translated
by Vladmír
Houdek and
Mac Hammond

Seven stars make music soar;
Each, in its own timbre and tone,
Sings, in tune, before God's throne,
Praising His beauty evermore.

The violin strings of the sun
Is a sunburst whose dazzling rays
Like a crown of stars, all one,
Shines toward heavenly pathways.

If the sun's bright violin string
Is, no, not enough for your ear,
Add the song of the moon's ring
And the symphony the stars hear.

When the sun, the moon, a star
Plays its violin, harp, or lute,
I want to be in heaven, far
From the earth and its earthly fruit.

Love is the music-master,
She herself, she tightens the strings,
Makes the music move faster,
And tries to give human hearts wings.

Listen well. How fine she sings!
Her beautiful music begins
And all of her effort wrings
Your heart with celestial violins.

157

TRIUMF, TRIUMF . . .

Václav
Karel
Holan
Rovenský
(1693)

Triumf, triumf, veselme se,
již victoria stala se,
silný s silným jest bojoval,
nad ďáblem zvítězil, vyhrál,
potlouk jej, křesťané, slavný král,
slavný král.

Kristus nahý, satan v zbroji,
že jest se strojil hned k boji,
prv zbodeného již čekal,
však on se nelekal,
s křížem, bez meče Ježíš ďábla flekal,
jej flekal.

Pekelné místo obloupil,
smrti i ďáblu na krk vstoupil,
věčně ukoval, svaté vzal,
plesejte, zpívejte, trubte,
bubnujte, zvítězil slavný král,
slavný král.

Všickni pekelní knížata
tarasovali hned vrata,
mníc, že obstojí v pokoji.
Však on polámal, roztřískal
závory pekelné, mocný král,
mocný král.

Zimu pryč zahnal, jarní čas,
půst pryč, nastal kvas, nastal kvas,
již po trápeni jest radost,
ženichům pouští se slavnost,
neb bývá po mračnu zas jasnost,
zas jasnost.

TRIUMPH, TRIUMPH . . .

Triumph, triumph! Joyfully
come celebrate a victory!
Mighty power has fought with power,
crushed the devil, conquering:
He has triumphed, glorious king,
glorious king.

Translated by
D. Gosselin
and A. French

Christ defenceless stood his ground,
Satan armed to strike Him down,
Yet He flinched not from the blow.
With the cross—no sword He bore—
Jesus beat the devil sore,
beat him sore.

Ransacked hell's infernal town,
bringing death and devil down,
spirited the saints away.
Sound the drums and trumpets; sing!
He hath triumphed, glorious king,
glorious king.

Every prince of hell in haste
rushed to barricade the gates,
thinking to survive the storm.
Down He broke them, splintering
gates of hell, the mighty king,
mighty king.

Spring has come, the winter ceased,
now the time to feast, to feast;
after sorrow radiant joy,
glory of the bridal days,
after darkness shining rays,
shining rays.

159

Hody se již začínají,
Beránka všickni jíst mají,
chudí, bohatí, žebráci,
kunstýři, učení žáci,
laikové, kněží i vojáci,
vojáci.

Ptáčkové se proletují,
čápi klektají na stodolách,
čížek, slavíček plesají,
„vít, vít" zpívajíc v pahrbkách
a v lesích, v hájcích, v polích i v horách,
i v horách.

Louky zelené koberce,
stromy rozvíjí praporce,
slunce radostí se směje,
bubnujíc voda se leje,
větříček libý sem tam věje,
tam věje.

Ejhle Beránek, přistupte,
bez stříbra, zlata jej kupte,
pekelné brány polámal,
rozbil, potlouk i roztřískal,
vám se bez obrany podal,
slavný král.

Buď'mež tedy jeho hosti,
když nás zůve k své slavnosti,
tak pojd'me všickni s radostí,
pospíchejme s ochotností,
budem s ním v věčné radosti,
v radosti.

Now the festival is come,
time for all to eat the Lamb,
poor and rich and beggar men,
artists, clerks, enlightened men,
laymen, priests and fighting men,
fighting men.

Across the sky the birds are flying,
from the barns the storks are crying,
nightingale and chaffinch dance.
Up aloft their twittering fills
groves and forests, fields and hills,
fields and hills.

Green the meadows' lush array,
trees unfurl their banners gay,
sunlight beams in glad delight,
as the drumming waters flow
eddying breezes softly blow,
softly blow.

Hail the Lamb! Christians, draw nigh!
Him no gold nor silver buy —
He that burst the gates of hell,
smashing, cracking, splintering,
now Himself the Offering,
glorious king.

Come, He bids us to His door
to enjoy His boundless store;
joy and gladness we shall draw
from His love for evermore.
Rejoice with Him for evermore,
evermore!

KDE JSTE, KDE . . .

Václav
Karel
Holan
Rovenský
(1693)

Kde jste, kde, císařové,
umřeli jste,
kde, světa mocnářové,
již víc nejste,
za vámi my půjdeme,
smrti neujdeme,
ach, půjdeme k vám do věčnosti.

Kde jste pak, kde, knížata,
zmizeli jste,
kde, přeslavná hrabata,
umřeli jste,
za vámi my půjdeme,
smrti neujdeme,
ach, půjdeme k vám do věčnosti.

Kde jste, krásné slečenky,
ach, zbledly jste,
kde, přepěkné panenky,
ach, shnily jste,
za vámi my půjdeme
smrti neujdeme,
ach, půjdeme k vám do věčnosti.

WHERE, WHERE ARE YOU . . .

Where, where are you, great emperors?
all dead and gone.
and where are you, earth's noble sirs?
your lives are done.
And we shall follow you
for death will claim us too.
Oh, we shall join you in eternity.

Translated by
A. French

O where are you, great lords of earth?
long since passed on.
And you, you men of noble birth?
dead and gone.
And we shall follow you,
for death will claim us too.
Oh, we shall join you in eternity.

And you, fair maid? your lovely face
turned white and cold,
You too, fine ladies, filled with grace?
rotting mould.
And we shall follow you,
for death will claim us too,
Oh, we shall join you in eternity.

163

Kde jste, statečné paní,
již nejste nic,
žádný vás již ze spaní
nezbudí víc,
za vámi my půjdeme,
smrti neujdeme,
ach, půjdeme k vám do věčnosti.

Kde jste, kde, boháčové,
ach, schudli jste,
kde světa miláčkové,
ach, ustydli jste,
za vámi my půjdeme,
smrti neujdeme,
ach, půjdeme k vám do věčnosti.

Kde jste, kde, i měštané,
ach, v kostnici,
jináče se nám nestane,
chtíc nechtíci
za vámi my půjdeme,
smrti neujdeme,
ach, půjdeme k vám do věčnosti.

Robotní sedláčkové
přestali jsou,
všichni hospodářové
již domů jdou,
za vámi my půjdeme,
smrti neujdeme,
ach, půjdeme k vám do věčnosti.

I my všickni na světě
tam půjdeme,
snad v tom neb v druhém létě,
tam, tam všickni půjdeme,
smrti neujdeme,
ach, půjdeme k vám do věčnosti.

O where are you, brave noblemen?
crumbled to dust,
and no one ever shall again
disturb your rest:
but we shall follow you,
for death will claim us too
Oh, we shall join you in eternity.

Where, where are you, the wealthy ones?
your wealth is fled.
And where are you, earth's favoured sons?
cold and dead;
and we shall follow you,
for death will claim us too.
Oh, we shall join you in eternity.

You city folk, where, where are you?
within the tomb,
and we ourselves, whate'er we do
must share your doom:
for we shall follow you,
and death will claim us too.
Oh, we shall join you in eternity.

The labours of the serfs are spent
at close of day;
the bailiffs all are homeward bent.
upon their way:
and we shall follow you,
for death will claim us too.
Oh, we shall join you in eternity.

All creatures of this worldly place
shall follow you,
this year, or in a little space,
we all, we all shall follow you:
for death will claim us too.
Oh, we shall join you in eternity.

During the second half of the eighteenth century there occurred in the Czech lands political, economic, and social changes which reacted sharply upon cultural life, and eventually upon literary production. With the official suppression of the Jesuit Order and the edict of religious toleration the period of the Counter-reformation was demonstratively concluded. The great processions and festivals of the church, with their magnificent trappings of gold, the flaming torches, rich apparel, incantation and music became a thing of the past. The baroque theatre combining poetry with music, the stately ballet with the magnificence of a contrived decor, disappeared from the palaces of the nobility, or else was changed out of recognition. With the enthronement of reason and the spread of enlightenment the other world had lost the terrors and mystery which had been the inspiration of baroque art. All over Western Europe the class which had regarded itself as the eternal guardian of power, truth, wisdom and tradition, now found itself an anachronism, typified by the Don Quixote of Cervantes. In the new climate of opinion and emotion a whole culture was swept aside, and in the Czech lands the new intellectuals deliberately cut themselves off from the preceding era, and sought to link up again with an older tradition. Regarding the century and a half since 1620 as a lost era in the development of a national culture, they resurrected the sixteenth century as a golden age of Czech literature, and saw in the folk song the surviving evidence of a cultural tradition which joined them to their past. In retrospect the whole era since the battle of the White Mountain seemed an age of darkness, from which the nation only now was emerging. The language of Europe diplomacy, higher education, and high literature had been Latin. The aristocracy of Bohemia had itself been more practised in German and French than in Czech; and in turning back to folk literature the earnest revivalists thought to find the purest source of their culture, lovingly preserved by simple peasants and uncontaminated by foreign sophistication. Thus was prepared the way for the nineteenth century Czech Romantic movement.

167

Předzpěw.

Ay zde ležj zem ta , před okem mým smutně slzjcjm,
  Někdy kolébka nynj národu mého rakew.
Stůg noho ! poswatné mjsta gsau kamkoli kráčjš ,
  K obloze , Tatry synu , wznes se wywýše pohled.
Neb raděgi k welikému přiwiň tomu tam se dubisku ,
  Genž wzdoruge zhaubným až dosawáde časům.
Wšak horšj ge času wzteklosti člowěk, genž berlu železnau
  Wtěchto kragjch na twau , Sláwie, šjgi chopil.
Horšj nežli diwé wúlky , hromu, ohně diwěgšj ,
  Zaslepenec , na swé když zlobu plémě lydá.
O wěkowé dáwnj , gako noc wůkol mne ležjcj ,
  O kragino welikié sláwy i hanby plná !
Od Lábe zrádného k rowinám až Wisly newěrné,
  Od Dunage k hltawým Baltu celého pěnám :
Krásnohlasý zmužilých Slowanů kde se někdy pzjwal ,
  Ay oněměl giž , byw k úrazu zášti , gazyk.
A kdo se laupeže té wolagjcj wzhůru dopustil?
    Kdo zhanobil w gednom národu lidstwo celé?
Zardi se záwistná Teutonie, sausedo Sláwy ,
  Twé win těchto počet spáchaly někdy ruky.
Sám swobody kdo hoden , swobodu zná wážiti každau ,
  Ten kdo do paut gjmá otroky, sám ge otrok.

A 2

In 1819 a Slovak protestant JAN KOLLÁR (1793-1852) returned to Prague from his studies at Jena University. Inspired there by the contemporary enthusiasm for romantic German nationalism, he wrote poetry proclaiming the ideal of an equally romantic Pan-slavism. His great work The Daughter of Slava, is a sequence of sonnets prefaced by a long invocation written in quantitive hexameters. The theme is a poetic pilgrimage through the home lands of the Slavonic people to the Slavic heaven and hell, with glimpses of the past great heroes of his people. Kollár's German sweetheart, to whom his first collection of poems had been addressed, is identified with the daughter of a Slavonic goddess; thus, as the mother spirit of the land, she embodies all its ideals and hopes. The whole work owes much in structure to Byron's Childe Harold, but its literary inspiration goes back to Petrarch and Dante, and beyond them to Virgil, and Greek mythology. The strength of the book lies in its Introduction, and some of its charming love sonnets: but on the whole it has a curiously archaic, not to say pedantic atmosphere, and some of the poems are so hard to understand that Kollár himself later published a work of notes and explanations to help the reader.

Like many writers Kollár will long be read, if not for the quality of his poetry, for the emotional and ideological content of his work. In the literary record he stands out as one of the first writers to proclaim that the tradition and destiny of the Czechs are part of a great vanished past of the Slav peoples. Czech poets thus saw their national revival as part of a historic movement.

169

PŘEDZPĚV

Jan
Kollár
(1793-1852)

Aj, zde leží zem ta před okem mým slzy ronícím,
  někdy kolébka, nyní národu mého rakev.
Stůj, noho! posvátná místa jsou, kamkoli kráčíš,
  k obloze, Tatry synu, vznes se, vyvýše pohled,
neb raději k velikému přichyl tomu tam se dubisku,
  jenž vzdoruje zhoubným až dosaváde časům.

Však času ten horší je člověk, jenž berlu železnou
  v těchto krajích na tvou, Slávie, šíji chopil.
Horší nežli divé války, hromu, ohně divější,
  zaslepenec na své když zlobu plémě kydá.
Ó věkové dávní, jako noc vůkol mne ležící,
  ó krajino, všeliké slávy i hanby obraz!
Od Labe zrádného k rovinám až Visly nevěrné,
  od Dunaje k hltným Baltu celého pěnám:
krásnohlasý zmužilých Slovanů kde se někdy ozýval,
  aj, oněmělt' už, byv k úrazu zášti, jazyk.

A kdo se loupeže té, volající vzhůru, dopustil?
  Kdo zhanobil v jednom národu lidstvo celé?
Zardi se, závistná Teutonie, sousedo Slávy,
  tvé vin těchto počet spáchaly někdy ruce,
neb krve nikde tolik nevylil černidlaže žádný
  nepřítel, co vylil k záhubě Slávy Němec.

Sám svobody kdo hoden, svobodu zná vážiti každou,
  ten kdo do pout jímá otroky, sám je otrok.
Necht' ruce, necht'by jazyk v okovy své vázal otrocké,
  jedno to, neb nezná šetřiti práva jiných.
Ten kdo trůny bořil, lidskou krev darmo vyléval,
  po světě nešt'astnou války pochodni nosil:
ten porobu slušnou, bud' Goth, bud' Skýta, zasloužil,
  ne kdo divé chválil příkladem ordě pokoj.

170

THE PRELUDE

Before my weeping eyes extends the land,
my people's cradle once, their coffin now.
Stir not, for where you tread is holy ground.
O Tatra's son, lift up your eyes to heaven,
or turn towards that mighty oak
which yet can spurn the ravages of time.

Translated
by Alfred
French

Yet worse than time is man, that in these lands
has fastened, Slav, upon your neck a yoke.
Still worse than fierce war, more fierce than fire
or thunder, is that blinded man who turns
in anger striking down his kin.
O ages past, around me like the night!
O land that mirrors all our pride and shame!
From traitor Elbe unto the eastern plains
that touch upon the faithless Vistula,
from Danube to the Baltic's gulping foam,
where once was heard the talk of Slavic men,
today that tongue, by hate oppressed, is still.
What nation bears the guilt for this, the deed
that struck one folk and tarnished all mankind?
Blush, envious Teuton, neighbour to the Slav
for all the crimes that lie upon your hands.
No enemy has shed such blood—or ink—
as Germany, to bring the Slav to grief.

Who honours freedom should himself be free;
who shackles others proves himself a slave;
and whether he confine men's hand or tongue,
he tramples equally upon the rights of man.
Who toppled thrones and squandered human blood,
who spread across the earth the chant of war,
—no matter be he Goth or Scythian—
such men are nature's slaves, not they
that showed barbarians the way to peace.

171

Kde jste se octly, milé zde bydlivších národy Slávů,
    národy, jenž Pomoří tam, tuto Sálu pily?
Sorbů větve tiché, Obodritské říše potomci,
    kde kmenové Vilců, kde vnukové jste Ukrů?
Napravo šíře hledím, nalevo zrak bystře otáčím,
    ncž mé darmo oko v Slávii Slávu hledá.

Rci, strome, chráme jejich rostlý, pode nímž se obětné
    dávnověkým tehdáž pálily žertvy bohům:
kde jsou národové ti, jejich kde knížata, města,
    jenž první v severu zkřisili tomto život?
Jedni učíce chudou Europu plachty i vesla
    chystati a k bohatým přes moře vésti břehům,
kov tu jiní ze hlubin stkvoucí vykopávali rudných,
    více ku poctě bohům nežli ku zisku lidem.
Tam ti neúrodné rolníku ukázali rádlem,
    by klas neslo zlatý, brázditi lůno země.
Lípy tito, svěcený Slávě strom, vedle pokojných
    cest sadili, chládek by stlaly vůkol i čich.
Muž syny města učil stavěti, v nich vésti kupectví,
    a mlad' svou učily tkávati plátno ženy.

Národe mistrovský, jakové pak máš za to díky?
    Rozškubaný hnusné zpotvořenosti věnec.
Jak včely med zavoníc kradné se do úle cizího
    stádně hrnou a pak matku i dítky bijí:
tak tu domu vlastní podroben pán, chytře mu vlezlý
    soused ovil těžký smutně o hrdlo řetěz.
Kde spanilá v zelených hájích pěla píseň Slovanka,
    už hlaholem zpěvná ústa umlkla němým.
Kde z mramoru stály hromného paláce Peruna,
    z troskotaných sloupů teď psota chlévy dělá.

Where are you now, dear Slavic folk that dwelt
beside the Baltic, and the Sala's stream?
the peaceful Sorbs? the Vilna tribes? the realm
of Obodrit? the sons of Uker's land?
From right to left I turn my eyes afar
in searching gaze across the Slavic lands
and seek in vain for Slavic Gloria.
Great tree, that temple rising from the earth,
beneath whose leafy boughs the offerings
to ancient gods arose in days of old—
Where are those cities, where their kings, the tribes
the first that called the Northern lands to life?
They taught benighted Europe how to sail,
to cross the sea in ships to richer shores.
They dug from depths of earth the shining ore,
the more to honour gods than profit men
They taught the husbandmen to plough the land
and mother earth to yield the golden corn.
They planted trees beside the quiet paths,
the noble linden, sacred to the Slav,
to spread its fragrant scent in cooling shade.
As mother taught her child to work the loom,
so son from father learned to build the towns
wherein their people plied their thriving trades.

Great nation, what was your reward for this?
a tattered wreath of horror and decay.
Like bees that infiltrate another's hive,
then swarming in, destroy the queen and young;
our neighbours wormed their way within the fold,
and then enslaved the master of the land,
and hung their heavy chains about his neck.
Where once the meadows rang with Slavic song,
today the haunting melodies are still.
Where once there rose the marble palaces,
the sacred shrines of the thunder god Perun,
now stand the beggared people's squalid huts
of salvaged wreckage from the chiselled stone.

173

KU BARBARŮM

Jan
Kollár

Ku barbarům rodu avarského
   přišli jednou trojí poslové,
   citary se k hudbě hotové
chvěly s jejich plece vysokého.
,Kdo jste?' chán k nim pyšně s trůnu svého,
   ,kde jsou vaše vojska, mečové?'
   ,,Pane," řeknou, ,,my jsme Slávové
ode krajin moře Baltického;
vojnu sotva podle jména známe,
   darmo žádáš od nás pomoci,
   my jen hru a zpěvy doma máme."
Hráli před ním, hráli přelíbezně,
   tyran na odměnu: ,Otroci,
   vlecte do zajetí tyto vězně!'

TO SAVAGE AVARS

To savage Avars in the days of old
came journeying three minstrels, in their hands
Slavonic harps with trembling strings they hold.
Upon his throne the haughty Khan demands

"What men are you? from what land do you ride?
"We are the Slavs, O lord," the bards replied,
"Our homelands verge upon the Baltic sea.

We know no wars—no arms to us belong
We cannot swell your regiments, O lord
our people's fancy is for play and song."

They played for him. They played so tenderly
the tyrant bade his slaves, as their reward,
"Lead off these men to close captivity."

Based on the
translation
of Sir John
Bowring

175

Josef Mánes

176

*K*ollár's younger contemporary, F. L. ČELAKOVSKÝ, equalled him in patriotism and in enthusiam for Slavic tradition. As a student he collected folk songs, and between 1822 and 1827 he published three volumes of Slavonic National Songs. In 1829 he published a book of poems modelled on the Russian, entitled Echoes from Russian Songs, followed by a volume of original work based on Czech folk-lore, Echoes from Czech Songs. Čelakovský is today celebrated less for his contribution to the study of folk-lore than for his adaptation of Russian epic verse in Czech, and above all for his graceful lyrics and ballads. No less intellectual and patriotic than Kollár, Čelakovský has a lighter touch; and his example helped to lead Czech poetry from the dangerous waters of academic historicism back to the stream of pure lyric.

177

ZIMNÍ

František
Ladislav
Čelakovský
(1799-1852)

Jak mi smutna přichází
    ta letošní zima,
jakoby se svět zakalil
    před očima mýma.

Všecky cesty, chodníčky
    sněhem zapadaly,
po kterých jsme jindy, milý!
    spolu chodívali.

Však je mi tak všelijak,
    všude mne to souží,
jedva že mi srdce z těla
    ven se nevytouží.

Je mi jako ptáčkovi,
    co na poli sedá,
a na sněhu, ubožátko,
    zrníčka si hledá.

Hledá, hledá zrníčka,
    ale nenachází:
tak mi také bez milého
    zima ta prochází.

178

WINTER SONG

How sad the winter seems this year,
The sombre winter days.
As if the world, before my eyes,
Were wrapped in misty haze.

Now every road and every path
Is blanketed with snow.
The paths where once we two, my love,
Together used to go.

And everywhere I feel myself
With weariness oppressed.
For yearning eats away my heart,
And tears it from my breast.

I feel just as a bird must feel
That settles on the ground,
And in the snow, poor creature, sits,
And looks for seeds around.

He looks, he looks for seeds around,
But never finds he one:
And so for me, without my love,
The winter cold comes on.

Translated
by Alfred
French

*I*n the poet K. H. MÁCHA Czech verse reached in one bound the high peak of western Romanticism—not the romanticism of the accomplished pastoral, but the nightmare world of mystery and horror, tormented souls, demon-haunted ruins, and moonlight falling on old graves. He is most famous for his long lyric-epic composition May, finished only a few months before his early death. The poem is organised in four cantos and includes two intermezzos. It opens in the pleasant and hopeful atmosphere of a Spring evening: the heroic Jarmila awaits the coming of her lover Vilém, the noble outlaw. The idyllic scene is darkened, first by the revelation of some dreadful episode in Jarmila's past, then, as a boat appears across the water, by the discovery that it contains not her lover, but a messenger with the news of his capture and imminent execution. In the second canto the scene is Vilém's prison, the dungeon by the lake. Here on the second night before his death he relives his past life. Driven out by his father, he was reared in a robber band, of which he became the leader. Because of love for Jarmila he killed her seducer, unaware that he was killing his own father. The moonlight streaming into the vault now emphasises the darkness around the castle, and the despair in the tortured mind of the prisoner. In the last canto Macha abandons the narrative-epic form and identifies himself as the narrator, who seven years after the execution, revisits the scene. It is again the season of May: the fragrance of Spring blossoms, the scented wind, the song of the birds, are filled with the promise of desire and love: upon the hill the skull is touched by the setting sun, as though crowned with a posy of roses. Love is no longer the courtly game of the mediaeval poet, or the intimate art of the rococo amoretti, but a storm of passion and unmentionable guilt which will end in the death or frenzy of its victims. The romantic poet, whose natural milieu was the haunted forest and the ruined vault, could contrast his yearning for the unattainable vistas of the imagination with his feeling of utter futility and despair.

As one of the great peaks of Czech literature May has been translated into English several times, but never with great success. The ambitious scope of the poem and its richly-worked style make it a formidable task for a translator.

181

MÁJ

(Druhý zpěv)

Karel Hynek
Macha
(1810-1836)

Klesla hvězda s nebes výše,
mrtvá hvězda siný svit;
padá v neskončené říše,
padá věčně v věčný byt.
Její pláč zní z hrobu všeho,
strašný jekot, hrůzný kvíl.
„Kdy dopadne konce svého?"
Nikdy - nikde - žádný cíl.
Kol bílé věže větry hrají,
při níž si vlnky šepotají.
Na bílé zdě stříbrnou zář
rozlila bledá lůny tvář;
však hluboko u věži je temno pouhé;
neb jasna měsíce světlá moc
uzounkým oknem u sklepení dlouhé
proletši se změni v pološerou noc.
Sloup sloupu kolem rameno si podává
temnotou noční. Z venku větru vání
přelétá zvražděných vězňů co lkání,
vlasami vězně pohrává.
Ten na kamenný složen stůl
hlavu o ruce opírá;
polou sedě a kleče půl
v hloub myšlenek se zabírá.
Po měsíce tváři jak mračna jdou,
zahalil vězeň v ně duší svou;
myšlenka myšlenkou umírá.

182

MAY

(Canto II)

Translated
by Stephen
Spender and
Karel Brušák

Fell a star from highest heaven,
Dead the star, a pallid gleam;
Falling through eternal spaces,
To her endless last abode.
Weeping from the grave of all things,
Shuddering her plaintive moan.
"When, then, will she end her falling?"
Never—nowhere—there's no goal.
Round the white tower play the winds,
Where below the soft waves whisper.
And the white wall coldly gleams
Silver pale in pale moon light;
Deep within the tower is dark
Where the bright power of the moon
Through long cells and narrow windows
Strangled, changes into night.
Pillars stretch to pillars shadowy
Arms through dark. The wind from outside
Howls within like the murdered captives,
Gently strokes the prisoner's hair.
He upon a bare stone table
Rests his head against his hands;
Half he sits and half is kneeling
Deeply buried in his thoughts.
In clouds moving slowly across the moon
The captive now conceals his soul;
Thought dies from ensuing thought.

183

„Hluboká noc! ty rouškou svou
ted' přikrýváš dědinu mou,
a ona truchlí pro mě! –
Že truchlí? – pro mě? – pouhý sen!
Ta dávno neví o mně.
Sotvaže zítra jasný den
nad její lesy vstane,
já hanebně jsem odpraven,
a ona – jak v můj první den –
vesele, jasně vzplane.“

Umlknul; po sklepení jen,
jenž nad sloupy se zdvíhá,
dál, dál se hlas rozlíhá;
až – jakby hrůzou přimrazen –
na konci síně dlouhé
usne v temnotě pouhé.
Hluboké ticho té temnosti
zpět vábí časy pominulé,
a vězeň ve snách dny mladosti
zas žije dávno uplynulé.
To vzpomnění mladistvých let
mladistvé sny vábilo zpět;
a vězně oko slzy lilo,
srdce se v citech potopilo; –
marná to touha v zašlý svět.

Kde za jezerem hora horu
v západní stíhá kraje,
tam – zdá se mu – si v temném boru
posledně dnes co dítko hraje.
Od svého otce v svět vyhnán,
v loupežnickém tam roste sboru.
Později vůdcem spolku zván,
dovede činy neslychané,
všude jest jméno jeho znané,
každémut': „Strašný lesů pán!“

184

"O thou deep night! who with thy veil
Now coverest my village home
Where I know she mourns for me!—
Mourns she?—for me?—a hollow dream!—
She did forget me long ago.
Tomorrow scarcely will bright day
Have risen over all her woods
Than I'll have died a shameful death.
And she—as in my earliest days—
Will joyfully gleam forth in the sun."

He ceased now; yet still through the cell
Lifted high on its pillars, echoed,
Re-echoed his voice, far and further,
Till it—as if transfixed with horror—
Lost wandering in the empty halls
Fell sleeping on dark emptiness.
The utter silence of this darkness
Recalls a long forgotten time,
The prisoner dreams of his young days
Scenes long past by, he lives again.
And the remembrance of those years
Recalls to him the dreams of boyhood;
And tears now fill his eyes, his heart
Overwhelms him in deep feelings;—
The vain desire for a past world.

Beyond the lake where mountain mountain
Succeeds, until the furthest West,
There—as he dreams—under dark pines
He plays again, once more a child.
His father drove him on the world,
Amongst robbers he grew to manhood.
Later, become head of the band,
He brought to pass unheard of deeds,
His name is famous everywhere,
All know: "The wild lord of the forests!"

185

Až posléz láska k růži svadlé
nejvejš roznítí pomstu jeho,
a poznav svůdce dívky padlé
zavraždí otce neznaného.
Protož jest u vězení dán;
a kolem má být odpraven
již zítra strašný lesů pán,
jak první z hor vyvstane den.
Ted' na kamenný složen stůl
hlavu o ruce opírá,
polou sedě a kleče půl
v hloub myšlenek se zabírá;
po měsíce tváři jak mračna jdou,
zahalil vězeň v ně duši svou,
myšlenka myšlenkou umírá.

„Sok—otec můj! vrah—jeho syn,
on svůdce dívky mojí!—
Neznámý mně.—Strašný můj čin
pronesl pomstu dvojí.
Proč rukou jeho vyvržen
stal jsem se hrůzou lesů?
Či vinu příští pomstí den?
Čí vinou kletbu nesu?
Ne vinou svou!—V života sen
byl jsem já snad jen vyváben,
bych ztrestal jeho vinu?
A jestliže jsem vůlí svou
nejednal tak, proč smrtí zlou
časně i věčně hynu?—
Časně i věčně?—věčně—čas—“
Hrůzou umírá vězně hlas
odražený od temných stěn;
hluboké noci němý stín
daleké kobky zajme klín,
a pamět' vězně nový sen.

186

Until, for love of a pale rose,
Vengeance inflamed him, and he, meeting
His love's betrayer, murdered
His father, whom he did not know.
For this he has been cast in prison;
And must be broken on the wheel
At dawn, the wild lord of the forests,
When first the light will climb the peaks.
He upon a bare stone table
Rests his head against his hands,
Half he sits and half is kneeling
Deeply buried in his thoughts;
In clouds moving slowly across the moon
The captive now conceals his soul,
Thought dies from ensuing thought.

"Rival—my father! Murderer—I,
His son. And he ravished my love!—
Unknown to me.—My violent deed
Will bring two-fold revenge on me.
Why, when cast out by him, should I
Become the terror of the woods?
And whose guilt will the dawn atone?
And whose guilt stuck on me a curse?
Not mine!—Was I within this dream
Of living, only lured perhaps
But to avenge my father's crime?
But if I had not willed the deed
Why must I then endure this death
Within time and for ever die?—
Within time, and for ever?—Ever—time—"
His voice now dies away with terror
Re-echoed by the darkened wall;
The silent shadows of deep night
Imprisoned in the narrow cell
Now fill his mind with a new dream.

187

„Ach—ona, ona! Anjel můj!
Proč klesla dřiv, než jsem ji znal?
Proč otec můj?—Proč svůdce tvůj?
Má kletba—"Léč hluboký žal
umoří slova. Kvapně vstal;
nocí řinčí řetězů hřmot,
a z mala okna vězně zrak
zalétá ven za hluky vod.—
Ouplný měsíc přikryl mrak,
než nade temný horní stín
vychází hvězdy v noci klín;
i po jezeru hvězdný svit,
co ztracené světlo se míhá.
Zrak vězně tyto jiskry stíhá,
a v srdce bolný vodí cit.
„Jak krásnát' noc! Jak krásný svět!
Jak světlo—stín se střídá!
Ach—zítra již můj mrtvý hled
nic více neuhlídá!
A jako venku šedý mrak
dál—dál se rozestírá:
tak—"Sklesl vězeň, sklesl zrak,
řetězů řinčí hřmot, a pak
u tichu vše umírá.
Již od hor k horám mraku stín—
ohromna ptáka perut' dlouhá—
daleké noci přikryl klín,
a šírou dálkou tma je pouhá.
Slyš! za horami sladký hlas
pronikl nocí temnou,
lesní to trouba v noční čas
uvádí hudbu jemnou.
Vše uspal tento sladký zvuk,
i noční dálka dřímá.
Vězeň zapomněl vlastních muk,
tak hudba ucho jímá.
„Jak milý život sladký hlas
v krajinu noční vdechne;
než zítřejší—ach—mine čas,
tu ucho mé ach nikdy zas
těch zvuků nedoslechne!"

"Ah—she! An angel! Mine! Why did
She fall, before we ever met?
Why, my father?—Seducing thee?
My curse—"Still deeper torment robs
Him of speech. Quickly he stood up;
The clattering chains aroused the night,
And through the window his wild gaze
Pierced far, to where the waters rustled.—
The clouds now covered the full moon.
Above the dark mountainous shadows
The lap of night was full of stars;
Their images trembling on the lake
Glimmered like quivering lost lights.
The prisoner gazed there where they sparkled
And sadness overcame his heart.
"O glorious night! O glorious world!
How light and shadow interweave!
At dawn already my dead gaze
Will see nothing—nothing—for ever!
Behold how the gray cloud outside
Draws near, and over, and withdraws!
Thus—"Fell the prisoner, fell his gaze,
The cold chains clattered, silence then
Encircled everything around.
Shadows of clouds from peak to peak—
Stretched like the span of giant wings—
Now cover the wide vale of night
And darkness fills afar the world.
Hark! From the mountains sweetest sound
Penetrates the dark. It is
The forest's horn, which through the night
Introduces tender music,
And all things slumber at its tune,
Even the dark horizons sleep.
So charms the tune the prisoner's ear
That he forgets his own deep pain.
"What lovely life the charming voice
Breathes into the sleeping landscape;
Before tomorrow—ah—has passed
My ear will have begun never,
Never to hear such sounds again!"

189

Zpět sklesne vězeň—řetěz hluk
kobkou se rozestírá;—
hluboké ticho.—V hloubi muk
se opět srdce svírá,
a dálné trouby sladký zvuk
co jemný pláč umírá.— —
,,Budoucí čas?!—Zítřejší den?!—
Co přes něj dál, pouhý to sen,
či spaní je bez snění?
Snad spaní je i život ten,
jenž žiji ted'; a příští den
jen v jiný sen je změní?
Či po čem tady toužil jsem,
a co neměla šírá zem,
zítřejší den mi zjeví?
Kdo ví?—Ach žádný neví—''

A opět mlčí. Tichá noc
kol kolem vše přikrývá.
Zhasla měsíce světlá moc,
i hvězdný svit, a kol a kol
je pouhé temno, šírý dol
co hrob daleký zívá.
Umlkl vítr, vody hluk,
usnul i líbý trouby zvuk,
a u vězení síni dlouhé
je mrtvé ticho, temno pouhé.
,,Hluboká noc—temná je noc!—
Temnější mně nastává— —
Pryč myšlenko!!''—A citu moc
myšlenku překonává.

Hluboké ticho.—Z mokrých stěn
kapka za kapkou splyne,
a jejich pádu dutý hlas
dalekou kobkou rozložen,
jako by noční měřil čas,
zní—hyne—zní a hyne—
zní—hyne—zní a hyne zas.

190

Backwards he sinks—the clattering chains May
Resound with iron through the cell;—
Then deep silence.—And then his heart
Is pierced through once more with that pain,
And far away the horn's sweet sound
Like tender weeping dies again.— —
"A future time?!.—Another day?!—
And after—what? Delusive dreams?
Or else a sleeping without dreams?
Perchance this life is also sleep,
This life of now; perhaps the dawn
Will only change to a new dream?
Or will that which I yearned for here,
That which the round earth never gave,
Perhaps be brought to me tomorrow?
Who knows?—Ah, no one can know this."

Silence again. The quiet night
Enshrouded everything around.
Extinguished now is the moon's brilliance
And glittering stars. The dark alone
Remains. The wide and spreading valley
Yawns like a deep enormous grave.
Silent the wind, silent the wave,
Asleep the lovely-sounding horn
And in the wide space of the cell
Is deathly stillness, dark, dark, dark.
"Deep is the night—and dark the night!—
Much greater darkness waits for me— —
Away, you thoughts!!"—Power of the heart
Now wins the victory over thought.

And silence—From the humid walls
Drop after drop falls after drop
And as they fall, the hollow sound
Echoes again in the long cell,
As if the drops were measuring time,
Resounds and dies—resounds and dies—
Resounding—dying—sound and death.

191

„Jak dlouhá noc—jak dlouhá noc—
Však delší mně nastává.— —
Pryč myšlenko!"—A hrůzy moc
myšlenku překonává.—
Hluboké ticho.—Kapky hlas
svým pádem opět měří čas.

„Temnějši noc!— —Zde v noční klín
ba lůny zář, ba hvězdný kmit
se vloudí— —tam—jen pustý stín,
tam žádný—žádný—žádný svit,
pouhá jen tma přebývá.
Tam všecko jedno, žádný díl—
vše bez konce—tam není chvil,
nemine noc, nevstane den,
tam času neubývá.—
Tam žádný—žádný—žádný cíl—
bez konce dál—bez konce jen
se na mne věčnost dívá.

Tam prázdno pouhé—nade mnou,
a kolem mne i pode mnou
pouhé tam prázdno zívá.—
Bez konce ticho—žádný hlas—
bez konce místo—noc—i čas— —
To smrtelný je mysle sen,
toť co se „nic" nazývá.
A než se příští skončí den,
v to pusté nic jsem uveden— — !"
Vězeň i hlas omdlívá.
A lehounce si vlnky hrají
jezerní dálkou pode věží,
s nimi si vlnky šepotají,
vězně uspávati se zdají,
jenž v hlubokých mrákotách leží.

192

"How long the night—how long the night—
Much longer night awaits for me.— —
Away, you thoughts!"—The power of terror
Now wins the victory over thoughts.
The silence deep. The sound of drops
Whose falling once more measures time.

"A deeper night!— —Here in the night
Starlight and moonlight oft appear— —
But there nothing—save empty shadows,
And there is never light—alone,
Ever-persisting, utter darkness.
There all is sameness, nothing separate—
There nothing ends—there is no instant,
Night does not cease nor day begin,
Time there never diminishes.—
And there is never aim nor goal,
Never an end—but endlessness,
Eternity there stares upon me.

There all is emptiness—above,
Around, and also under me.
Yawns blankness, blankness everywhere—
And silence without end—speechless—
And space without end—night—time— —
And thus thought dreams of mortal things
That is the thing that's nothing called
Before tomorrow will have passed
Into that nothing I'll be thrown— —!"
He falls back fainting speechlessly.
The little waves play now so lightly
In the white lake beneath the tower,
And little waves whisper with them,
They seem to lull to sleep the captive
Who now lies bound in a deep trance.

Strážného vzbudil strašný hřmot,
jejž řetězů činí padání;
se světlem vstoupil.—Lehký chod
nevzbudil vězně z strašných zdání.
Od sloupu k sloupu lampy svit
dlouhou zalétá síní,
vždy bledší—bledší její kmit,
až vzadu zmizí její moc,
a pustopustá temná noc
ostatní díl zastíní.

Leč nepohnutý vězně zrak—
jak by jej ještě halil mrak—
zdá se, že nic nezírá;
ač strážce lampy rudá zář
ubledlou mu polila tvář,
a tma již prchla čírá.
On na kamenný složen stůl
hlavu o ruce opírá,
polou sedě a kleče půl
znovu v mdlobách umírá;
a jeví hlasu šepot mdlý,
že trapnýt' jeho sen i zlý.

„Duch můj—duch můj—a duše má!"
Tak slova mu jednotlivá
ze sevřených ust plynou.
Než však dostihne ucho hlas,
tu slova strašná ničím zas—
jakž byla vyšla—hynou.

Přistoupí strážce, a lampy zář
před samou vězně vstoupí tvář.
Obličej vězně—strašný zjev—
oko spočívá nehnuté
jak v neskončenost napnuté,
po tváři slzy—pot a krev;
v ustech spí šepot—tichý zpěv.

194

The watchman woke at the wild noise
Of the loud fall of heavy chains;
He brought a light.—His soft footfall
Did not disturb the prisoner's nightmare.
Pillar to pillar fled the light
Of the lamp through the narrow room,
But paler always grew the flickering
Till in the corners it had vanished
And there in heavy shadowed space
Was only dark and empty night.

And yet the prisoner's rigid stare—
As if black clouds enveloped him—
Appeared as though he saw no longer;
This even when the watchman's lamp
Poured crimson rays upon his face
And scattered with its light the shadows.
He on a stone table resting
Leans his head against his hands,
Half he sits and half is kneeling,
Sunk again in a deep trance;
And whispering his voice now utters
The evil torment of his dream.

"My spirit—spirit—and my soul!—"
Thus one by one do the words fall
From lips compressed with bitter anguish.
Before his voice reaches the ear,
The dreadful words have died away—
As they have come—so do they perish.

The watchman draws close and now the rays
Reached to the captive's countenance.
That countenance—so terrible—
The eyes that stare, fixed, motionless,
As if fixed on endlessness,
On his face tears, and sweat, and blood:
On lips sleep whispers—a silent song.

195

Tu k ustům vězně ucho své
přiklonil strážce bázlivé;
a jak by lehký větřík vál,
vězeň svou pověst šepce dál.
A strážný vzdy se níž a níž
ku vězni kloní—blíž a blíž,
až ucho s usty vězně spojí.
Ten šepce tíše—tíš a tíš,
až zmlkne—jak by pevně spal.

Leč strážný nepohnutě stojí,
po tváři se mu slzy rojí,
ve srdci jeho strašný žal.—
Dlouho tak stojí přimrazen,
až sebrav sílu kvapně vstal,
a rychlým krokem spěchá ven.
On sice—dokud' ještě žil—
co slyšel, nikdy nezjevil,
než navždy bledé jeho líce
neusmály se nikdy více.

Za strážným opět temný stín
zahalil dlouhé síně klín;
hlubokou nocí kapky hlas
svým pádem opět měřil čas.
A vězeň na kamenný stůl
složený—klečí—sedí půl.
Obličej jeho—strašný zjev—
oko spočívá nehnuté,
jak v neskončenost napnuté,
po tváři slzy—pot—a krev.

A ustavičně kapky hlas
svým pádem dále měří čas.
A kapky—vod i větrů zpěv
vězňovi blízký hlásá skon,
jenž myšlenkami omdlívá.—
Z dálky se sova ozývá,
a nad ním půlnoc bije zvon.

Afraid, the watchman leans his ear
Against the prisoner's mouth; as if
A light breeze stirred there, softly
The prisoner breathes his tale.
The watchman bends down deep and deeper
Towards the prisoner—near and nearer,
Until his ear joins to that mouth
Which whispers softly—softly, softly,
Till it is dumb—as though asleep.

The watchman stands fast, motionless,
And on his cheeks the tears pour down,
And in his heart is dreadful grief.—
He stands long, as if rooted there,
At last he tears himself away,
And with swift step hastens outside.
Though he—in all his years of life—
Never betrayed what he then heard,
Yet afterwards his hollow cheeks
Have never smiled—never again.

Behind the watchman the dark shadows
Darkened once more the narrow cell;
Through the deep night the sounding drops
Measured again time in their fall.
And there the prisoner upon the table
Resting—kneeling—and half seated.
His countenance—terrible picture—
His eyes that stay quite motionless,
As if fixed on endlessness,
On his face tears, and sweat, and blood.
And endless sounding of the drops
In their fall still measuring time.
And drops—and waves, and breezes tell
The captive of his nearing end
He faints powerless from his thoughts.—
From far the own calls, and over him
The clock now strikes the midnight hour.

197

esem vám
noviny
poslouchejte,
z Betlemské
krajiny
pozor dejte!

a t:d:

Mikoláš Aleš

198

*I*n his own country Mácha's work did not win immediate acclaim, in spite of his later influence. In the literary record there is a curious hiatus after his name, for he had no immediate successors. The trend for the coming generation of writers was set rather by his contemporary, the poet and folklorist K. J. ERBEN. Whereas the strength and appeal of Mácha lies in his spirit of revolt, annihilation and despair—essentially the spirit of the revolutionary in art—the appeal of Erben lies in his spirit of continuity, linking his own generation of the literary renaissance with traditions whose charm was their age and familiarity. If Mácha was charged by his contemporaries with a lack of national spirit, the same could not be said of Erben, who sought in his work for what he romantically conceived as the essence of the national consciousness, preserved in the life of the common folk.

His position as an archivist gave him abundant opportunity to develop his researches into the art of folk poetry and music, and in his early years he published an anthology which became a classic of its kind. In the course of his official duties at the museum he transcribed, edited and published a series of Old Czech literary documents, and acquired an enormous breadth of knowledge of Czech history and tradition at a secondary level. One result of his work was the publication in 1864 of his collection of more than 2,000 folk songs. By his work Erben not only rescued much traditional poetry from oblivion, but established for the folk song an honored and secure place in the Czech literary record.

Erben used his erudition and mastery of folk-lore technique in the ballads which he wrote himself. His themes were drawn from traditional folk myth, but the ballads themselves were models of sophisticated art, repeatedly revised and improved, as we know from the surviving manuscripts of his successive drafts.

ŠTĚDRÝ DEN

I

Karel Jaromír
Erben
(1811-1870)

Tma jako v hrobě, mráz v okna duje,
v světnici teplo u kamen;
v krbu se svítí, stará podřimuje,
děvčata předou měkký len.

,,Toč se a vrč, můj kolovrátku!
ejhle adventu již nakrátku,
a blizko, blizoučko Štědrý den!,,

Mílotě děvčeti přísti, mílo
za smutných zimních večerů;
neb nebude darmo její dílo,
tu pevnou chová důvěru.

I přijde mládenec za pilnou pannou,
řekne: ,,Pojď za mne, dívko má!
budiž ty mi ženkou milovanou,
věrným ti mužem budu já.

CHRISTMAS EVE

I

An icy wind—night black as the grave—
warm glows the fire within:
an aged woman nods by the hearth
and the maidens softly spin.

"O turn, my spinning wheel, and hum,
soon Advent will be past,
and Christmas here at last."

A maiden's joy it is to spin
through the chilly winter evening;
reward one day will crown her toil,
she firmly trusts, believing

a youth will come for the busy maid,
and say "O follow me:
come, be my darling wife, and I
your faithful man will be.

Translated
by Alfred
French

201

Já tobě mužem, ty mně ženkou,
dej ruku, děvče rozmilé!"—
A dívka, co předla přízí tenkou,
svatební šije košile.

"Toč se a vrč, můj kolovrátku!
však jest adventu již nakrátku,
a přede dveřmi Štědrý den!"

II.

Hoj, ty Štědrý večere,
ty tajemný svátku!
cože komu dobrého
neseš na památku?

Hospodáři štědrovku,
kravám po výslužce,
kohoutovi česneku,
hrachu jeho družce.

Ovocnému stromovi
od večeře kosti,
a zlatoušky na stěnu
tomu, kdo se postí.

"Hoj, já mladá dívčina,
srdce nezadané:
mně na mysli jiného,
jiného cos tane.

Pod lesem, ach pod lesem,
na tom panském stavě,
stojí vrby stařeny,
sníh na šedé hlavě.

Jedna vrba hrbatá
tajně dolů kývá,
kde se modré jezero
pod ledem ukrývá.

202

"O give your hand to me, my love,
our troth with joy we'll crown;
and the maid who spun the tender flax
will spin a wedding gown."

"O turn, my spinning wheel, and hum,
soon Advent will be past,
and Christmas here at last."

II

O welcome, Christmas Eve, in all
your holy mystery:
what gifts to everyone you bring
for Christmas memory?

The farmer gets his plaited bread,
the cattle their reward;
the rooster, garlic; peas for hens;
to each his favourite food.

The fruit trees will receive the bones
from yesternight's repast;
and golden sucklings on the wall
feed eyes of those who fast.

"O I am yet a maiden young,
my heart is fancy free.
But the strangest feeling haunts my mind,
and seems to beckon me.

"Within the wood, within the wood,
in the manor park there grow
two very aged willow trees;
their heads are grey with snow.

"One gnarled willow nods and bends
toward the lake below,
where underneath the spreading ice
the hidden waters flow.

203

Tu prý dívce v půlnoci,
při luně pochodni,
souzený se zjeví hoch
ve hladině vodní.

Hoj, mne půlnoc neleká,
ani liché Vědy:
půjdu, vezmu sekeru,
prosekám ty ledy.

I nahlednu v jezero
hluboko—hluboko,
milému se podívám
pevně okem v oko."

III.

Marie, Hana, dvě jména milá,
panny jak jarní růže květ;
která by z obou milejší byla,
nikdo nemůže rozumět.

Jestliže jedna promluví k hochu,
do ohně by jí k vůli šel;
pakli se druhá usměje trochu—
na první zas by zapomněl!—

Nastala půlnoc. Po nebi šíře
sbor vysypal se hvězdiček,
jako ovečky okolo pastýře,
a pastýř jasný měsíček.

Nastala půlnoc, všech nocí máti,
půlnoc po Štědrém večeru;
na mladém sněhu svěží stopu znáti
ode vsi přímo k jezeru.

204

"And here, they say, when midnight strikes,
by the moon's uncertain beam
a maiden sees her fated man
on the surface of the stream.

"Then I who fear not midnight's spell
nor what false prophets say,
will go, and take the axe with me,
and cut the ice away.

"Then I will look into the lake
deep, deep beneath the ice.
And I will see my lover there
and gaze into his eyes."

III

Marie and Hannah, two sweet names,
like Spring flowers undefiled:
and none could tell which of the two
was e'er the lovelier child.

A word from one girl to a youth
would set his heart aflame:
The other smiled—at once the youth
forgot the first girl's name. . . .

So midnight came: across the sky
stars shining through the gloom,
as round a shepherd stand the sheep:
the shepherd was the moon.

So midnight came, that night of nights,
the night of Christmastide;
upon the snow a footprint points
toward the waterside.

205

Ta jedna klečí, nad vodou líčko;
ta druhá stojí podle ní:
"Hano, Haničko, zlaté srdíčko!
jaké tam vidíš vidění?"

" "Ach vidím domek—ale jen v šeře—
jako co Václav ostává—
však již se jasní—ach, vidím dvéře,
ve dveřích mužská postava!" "

" "Na těle kabát zeleni temné,
klobouk na stranu—znám jej, znám!
na něm ta kytka, co dostal ode mne—
můj milý bože! Václav sám!!" "

Na nohy skočí, srdce jí bije;
druhá přikleká vedle ni:
" "Zdař bůh, má milá, zlatá Marie!
jaké ty vidíš vidění?" "

"Ach vidím, vidím—je mlhy mnoho,
všecko je mlhou zatmělé;
červená světla blýskají z toho—
zdá mi se býti v kostele."

"Něco se černá mezi bílými—
však mi se rozednívá již:
jsou to družičky, a mezi nimi—
pro boha! rakev—černý kříž!"

* * *

V.

Nastala zima, mráz v okna duje,
v světnici teplo u kamen;
v krbu se svítí, stará polehuje,
děvčata zase předou len.

206

The one girl kneels above the ice,
and next to her, Marie:
"O Hannah, Hannah, dearest heart,
what vision do you see?"

"I see a cottage—very faint,
like Václav's home, I swear,
more clearly now—I see a door—
a man is standing there.

"He wears a jacket, dark and green,
a hat—well known to me—
and in the hat the flower I gave,
sweet Jesu! it is he!"

Then up she springs with racing heart;
Marie kneels next to her:
"God bless you, Marie dear, my love,
what vision see you there?"

"I see, I see—through a veil of mist,
in the gloom, obscurely,
some flicking lights of red—it seems,
like the chapel sacristy.

"Some white is there—a patch of black—
at last I see its shape;
a group of bridesmaids, and—O God!
a coffin decked with crepe!"

* * *

V

Another winter: icy winds;
warm glows the fire within.
An aged woman bends by the fire,
and the maidens softly spin.

"Toč se a vrč, můj kolovrátku!
však jest adventu zase na krátku,
a nedaleko Štědrý den!"

"Ach ty Štědrý večere
noci divoplodné!
když si na tě vzpomenu,
k srdci mne to bodne!"

"Seděly jsme také tak
loni pohromadě:
a než rok se obrátil,
dvě nám chybí v řadě!"

"Jedna, hlavu zavitou,
košiličky šije;
druhá již tři měsíce
v černé zemi hnije,
ubohá Marie!"

"Seděly jsme také tak
jako dnes a včera:
a než rok se obrátí,
kde z nás bude která?"

"Toč se a vrč, můj kolovrátku!
všeckoť ve světě jen na obrátku,
a život lidský jako sen!"

"Však lépe v mylné naději sníti,
před sebou čirou temnotu,
nežli budoucnost odhaliti,
strašlivou poznati jistotu!"

"O turn, my spinning wheel, and hum,
soon Advent will be past,
and Christmas here at last.

"How full of mystery they are,
the nights of Christmas Eve!
Oh, when I think of years gone by,
my heart is stabbed with grief.

"For here we sat, a year ago,
the group of us together;
and before the year had run its course
two were gone forever.

"The one bent over baby clothes
and sewing busily;
the other laid below the earth
to rot eternally.
Poor Marie!

"And here we sat, a year ago
like only yesterday:
and before another year has passed,
who yet will pass away?

"O turn, my spinning wheel, and hum,
for nothing on earth can last,
and life, like a dream, flies past.

"But better dream, with empty hopes,
in blind uncertainty,
than pierce the veil that hides the face
of fearful destiny."

209

Karel Havliček Borovský by Adolf Hoffmeistr

*B*oth Mácha and Erben, in their different ways, were spokes-
men of that romantic nationalism which, when carried into the
political field, culminated in the fighting at the barricades in
Prague of 1848. There the dreams of national autonomy and Slav
unity crumpled before the realities of political power. In many
Czech homes the tasselled swords and gay cockades of revolt were
quietly put away to await better days. Political disillusionment in
public life coincided with a shift in taste in popular literature. As
the Romantics had written in reaction against the dry asceticism of
the Enlightenment so in its turn romanticism gave way to a wave
of cynical, realistic and epigrammatic literature of which the
best-known poetic representative is probably KAREL HAVLIČEK-
BOROVSKÝ (1821-56). A political journalist who was dismissed
and exiled for his nationalist attitudes. Havliček was a poet of
distinction. He is perhaps best known for his long satiric poem,
the epic parody entitled, The Baptism of St. Vladimir.

211

KAREL HAVLÍČEK BOROVSKÝ:
KŘEST
SV. VLADIMÍRA/

Zpěv prvý

PERUN A VLADIMÍR

Karel
Havlíček
Borovský
(1821-1856)

Vladimír cár na svůj svátek,
když seděl na trůnu,
poslal drába s vyřízením
k bohovi Perunu.

„Hřmi, Perune, na můj svátek
místo kanonády,
škoda prachu, dost ho padne
v bitvách u armády.

212

THE BAPTISM OF ST. VLADIMIR

Canto I

Perun and Vladimir

Tsar Vladimir in his palace,
On his natal day,
Sent a sergeant of policemen
To Perun to say:

"Thunder, Lord Perun, this evening,
In place of cannon fire;
Spare our powder, shot and ordinance
And our soldiers' hire.

Translated
by William
Harkins

Hřmi, Perune, na můj svátek
místo kanonády,
pak si přijdi se mnou vypít
šálek čekolády." —

Pan dráb přišel k Perunovic,
zatloukl na vrata,
děvečky se hnedle zeptal:
„Doma-li pantáta?"

„Doma, doma, pane drábe,
ve veliké chatě,
sedí s jehlou na pekýlku,
zašívá si katě."

„Vzkazuje vás, pantatinku,
cár náš pozdravovat,
máte prej mu k tomu svátku
drobet zabubnovat."

Jak to přeslech tatík Perun,
hnedle čelo zvraštil,
skočil s kamen na lavici,
kat'mi o zem praštil:

"Thunder, good Perun, this evening,
In place of cannon fire;
Later come and drink some chocolate,
If you aren't too tired."

Our good sarge went to Perun's house,
Pounded with a din,
Asked the housemaid when she opened
If he might come in?

"Come in, Sarge, the master's home now,
In the parish manse,
In the kitchen on the stovetop,
Sewing up his pants."

"I am sent by Tsar Vladimir:
Your help is besought:
If you thunder for his birthday,
We can save on shot."

Perun heard no sooner than he
Broke into a roar,
Threw his pants down in a choler,
Jumped down to the floor.

215

„Ráděj pásat husy ve vsi,
po bahnách se ploužit,
než u toho Vladimíra
zde za boha sloužit.

Málo platu, služba těžká,
nikdy konec práce,
ještě bych mu měl vyvádět
ve svátek regrace?

Tuhle při poslední bouřce,
při té blýskavici,
beztoho jsem si propálil
celou nohavici!

Málo platu, málo športlí,
málo deputátu!
Nemohu si špendýrovat
oleje k salátu!

Pečínku jenom ve svátek,
vodu musím píti,
sotva jsem se na tu službu
mohl oženiti.

Beztoho mne větším dílem
živí jen kondice,
študentům hodiny dávat
musím ve fyzice.

Kdyby od selek nekáplo
trochu akcidence,
ani v neděli bych nemoh
přičuchnout k pálence!

Pro nic za nic robotovat—
nevěděl bych věru,
na tu jeho čekoládu,
že mu na ní seru!

216

"Rather let me be a swineherd,
Eating nought but swill,
Than to be a tsar's factotum,
Subject to his will.

"Lousy pay, and too much backache,
And no end to woe,
When you've got to spend your days off,
Getting up a show.

"Just the other day I got caught
In a thunderstorm,
Dropped a bolt and burned the seat out
Of my uniform.

"Lousy pay and very little
In the way of tips!
All God can afford to eat is
Beer, salt fish and chips!

"Roastbeef only on a Sunday,
It's a lousy life!
Only with her pa's help can I
Afford to keep a wife.

"For my living I give lessons,
Make the students cram,
Teach them high-school physics for their
College board exam.

"If the perks from peasant clients
Weren't still coming in,
I'd be quite unable now to
Have a drop of gin.

"Drudgery, and all for nothing,
For the higher brass;
And that lousy invitation—
Stick it up your ass!

Cár necár, svátek nesvátek,
že mi všechno rovno,
ne a ne a nebudu hřmít,
co z toho mám? Hovno!"–

Dráb stál celý zkoprnělý
jako kapr v žitě:
,,Pamatujte se, pantáto,
copak to mluvíte?

Já jsem taky jen služebník,
každý zná své meze,
kdybych to vyřídil cáru,
co se na vás sveze?"–

Ale Perun, jak byl v ráži,
sáhnul pod lavici
a vytáh na pana drába
tu svou hromovnici.

Dráb se dlouho nezdržoval,
hledal honem díru
a hned běžel jak s keserem
k cáru Vladímíru:

,,Jdu Vašemu Veličenstvu
slušně vomeldovat,
že se to, co mluvil Perun,
stydím opakovat.

At' si tu svou čekoládu
cár prej sám sežere,
a že on na celou službu
s odpuštěním sere;

že je cáruv svátek a prd
s odpuštěním rovno,
že mu je po celém cáru
s odpuštěním hovno!"– –

"I don't give a clipped brass farthing
For your copper's star—
I won't thunder—say that's final,
When you see the tsar!"

Stupefaction showed all over
Our good sergeant's face.
"Mind your manners, Daddy Perun,
Or you'll lose your place.

"I am just obeying orders,
Don't make such a row;
Just suppose I told our sovereign
What you said just now?"

But Perun was so excited
That he stopped to pick
Up from underneath the cupboard
His stout thunderstick.

Sarge was not disposed to dally,
Hastening to get out;
His return trip to the palace
Looked more like a rout.

"I return to stand, Your Highness,
Humbly at your feet;
What Perun replied to you I
Hardly dare repeat.

"He sends back your invitation,
Says you've got some brass:
That Your Grace can take and stick it—
Pardon—up your ass.

"And about Your Royal Highness
He said some awful word:
That Your Grace is—beg your pardon—
Nothing but a turd."

Jak uslyšel Vladimír cár
tohle grobiánstvo,
plivnul na zem, zasakroval,
a s ním všechno panstvo.

Poslal čtyry policajty
k bohovi Perunu:
„Přiveďte ho, grobiána,
ku cárskému trůnu!"

A když vyšli policajti,
pískl na ně oknem:
„Hej, nechte to až do zejtřka,
my v suchu nezmoknem.

Však my se ho o ty jeho
hromy neprosíme,
pokud máme své kanóny,
sami si zahřmíme!"

Poslal flügel-adjutanta
pro dvě baterie,
ať bouchají při tabuli,
když se zdraví pije.

Jedli, pili, hodovali,
hrály jim muziky,
ministři si popouštěli
u kalhot knoflíky.

Pili pivo, pili víno,
jedli z masa, z těsta,
nejednomu oficíru
pukla z toho vesta.

Kdo při tom byl, ten se opil,
blaze, braši, tomu,
v noci je pak s výslužkami
roznášeli domů.

220

When Vladimir heard this answer,
He cursed his man and swore;
He and all his suite of nobles
Spat upon the floor.

Four policemen he commanded
To arrest Perun:
"He'll learn, wretch, to mend his ways and
Sing a different tune."

But at once he thought it better
After them to say,
"Come back; it can keep till morning,
He won't get away!"

"We can do without his thunder,
It's a bloody bore:
When we've got our own artillery—
Let the cannons roar!"

So he sent an aide to muster
His artillery
Cannons boomed in noisy concert
For their revelry.

'Gainst sobriety and moderation
There were, I fear, offenders;
All the ministerial council
Loosened their suspenders.

Savories they ate and sweet foods,
Wine they drank and stout;
More than one court officer
Split his waistcoat out.

They became intoxicated,
Theirs—a happy day!
Late at night their household servants
Carried them away.

221

Zpěv drubý

HOSPODÁŘSTVÍ

Jedna hora vysoká je
a druhá je nízká,
kdo nemá své muzikanty,
na hubu si píská.

Když hýřili, stolovali
u cárského dvoru,
ten celý den byl bůh Perun
v mrzutém humoru.

„Kdo jaktěživ bohem nebyl,
zkusil ještě málo,
není to tak lehký život,
jako by se zdálo.

Ráno vstane, do snídaně
musí rosou kropit,
měsíčka zavřít do chlívka,
potom v slunci topit.

Dříve čerty, noční duchy
strčit do pytlíka
a hvězdičky put'-t'u-t'u-t'u
svolat do kurníka.

Každý ptáček, každý brouček,
slon až do komára —
má hned ráno nasypáno
z božího špejchara.

A když potom lidi vstanou,
to je teprv správa!
Někdy nevím samým křikem,
kde mi stojí hlava.

Canto II

How the World Is Kept Going

One green mountain can be lofty,
While another's low;
One who can't give feasts can grumble
So that all may know.

While they revelled and they feasted
In Vladimir's courts,
Lord Perun was all the day long
Wholly out of sorts.

"One who's never had experience
Hardly can perceive
That a god's life's not so easy
As one might believe.

"Early up, before his breakfast,
He must sprinkle dew,
Lock the moon up in the cowshed,
Stoke the sunball, too.

"Then the demons he must gather
In a sack to stick,
And the stars be put to roosting,
Calling, 'Chick-chick-chick.'

"Every birdling, every beetle,
Elephant and fish,
Must at once have provender
Set out in a dish.

"And when human beings waken,
That's the final straw!
With their bawling and their chatter
One can't hear at all!

223

Ten, kdo nikdy neměl v uchu
vosy a brabence,
neví, co je Perunova
ranní audience.

To je křiku a modlení,
až mne uši brní:
ten zpívá, ten šepce, vzdychá,
ten zas žalmy frní.

A co všechno na mně chtějí,
nelze vyjmenovat,
zbláznil bych se, kdybych si to
měl jen pamatovat.

Ten chce zdraví, ta chce děti,
ten nemá co jísti,
ti zas, abych nedovolil
ve fabrikách přísti.

Ten chce zimu, ten chce teplo,
ten zas časy jiné,
jeden chce mít žito drahé
a druhý laciné.

Jeden sedlák prosí o dešť,
zasel kousek lenu;
druhý prosí hezké časy,
by měl sucho k senu.

Že jsem stvořil staré báby,
to mne nejvíc mrzí,
nepřestanou-li mne soužit,
zahladím je brzy.

Hrom ať do nich, abych neklel,
zdržet se nemohu!
když jí koza málo dojí,
běží k pánu bohu.

"If you've never had an earful
Of black wasps and ants,
You won't know how to imagine
Perun's audience.

"It's a mad concatenation:
Bellows, groans and yells,
Whispering, singing, sighing,
Prayers and magic spells.

"And the things they ask of me now
No one could recall;
I'd go mad if I were made to
Memorize it all.

"One wants health, another children,
Some want a life of ease;
Some petition me to outlaw
Spinning factories.

"One wants cold, another hot spells,
Some want only rain;
One wants meat to be expensive,
And another grain.

"One demands a heavy rainfall:
He's sown a field of rye;
One inveighs against damp weather
So his hay can dry.

"That I fashioned those old women—
That's my worst vexation;
If they don't stop I'll subject them
To extermination.

"Thunder strike all peasant women
Without more delay:
If their cattle start to dry up
They plop down to pray.

225

Sám se nechce žádný starat,
o všechno se modlí,
jako by měl každý boha
jen pro své pohodlí.

Tomu sušit, tomu močit,
tomu pole hnojit,
dřív si, prase, zdraví zkazil,
potom ho mám zhojit!

Ta mne moří ve dne v noci,
ráda by se vdala,
ten se modlí, by Morena
jeho ženu vzala.

Ten chce výhru z loterie,
špendáže mi nosí,
a co jsou asekurace,
též o oheň prosí!

Ó vy šelmy, kdybych nebyl
příliš dobrotivý,
zmačkal bych vás na povidla
jako zhnilé slivy!"— —

Pozdě v noci, když utich svět
a lid přestal bouřit,
chtěl si Perun usoužený
dýmčičku vykouřit.

„Však jsem já dobře slyšela
za dveřmi skrz škvíru,
co jsi vzkázal po drábovi
cáru Vladimíru.

Nezačínej si jen s cárem,
to já pořád říkám,
že to se svou opozicí
nepřivedeš nikam.

"No one takes the trouble now to
Do it for himself;
Each proclaims his right to ask for
God's unending help.

"Peasants beg that I should cover
Their fields with manure;
Some neglect their health for pleasure—
I have them to cure!

"One old maid torments me ever:
She would like to marry;
One old man would rid himself of
His wife who's contrary.

"One brings gifts so that I'll help him
Win a lottery;
One wants fire so he'll collect on
His new policy.

"Oh, you scoundrels! If it were that
I were hard to suit,
I would crush you to a jelly
Like old rotten fruit."

When at last he got a respite,
It was very late,
But his sleep was interrupted
By his peevish mate.

"I heard all your conversation
Listening through a crack:
How you swore at Tsar Vladimir,
And the answer you sent back.

"Disagreeing with Vladimir
Won't help your position;
You'll get nowhere as a member
Of the opposition.

Každému do očí řekneš,
co máš na jazyku,
a děláš si nepřátele,
nemáš politiku."

A když žena po celý den
bručí jen a štěká,
och, to musí z kůže vyhnat
boha i člověka!

Oj Perune, kam jsi myslil,
přenešťastný bůže?
Utec, utec, jak tě chytnou,
nic ti nepomůže!

Zpěv třetí

VOJENSKÝ SOUD

Bože, kýž jsem policajtem,
to je vyražení,
koho chce, toho si chytne
a dá do vězení.

Každý si ho musí vážit;
kdo naň zaškaredí,
pro urážku policajta
ve štokhauzu sedí.

Ctěte, hoši, policajty!
Ouvej, jak to bolí,
stát vyplácí krejčím metlou,
ale ševcům holí.

Slyšte, lidi, pro výstrahu
mé smutné zpívání,
že se proti policajtům
sám bůh neubrání.

228

"Blurt out all that comes to mind and
Then you can't retract:
That way you'll make enemies.
You've got no sense of tact!"

When a wife will blame her husband,
Nagging him and mumbling,
She can drive a man half-crazy
With her constant grumbling.

Ah, Perun, Perun, my brother,
What now will you do?
Flee from here, for once they catch you,
None can rescue you.

Canto III

The Court-Martial

Lord, if I were a policeman,
That would be great fun:
A policeman can imprison
Almost anyone.

Everyone respects policemen;
At them no one jeers:
For an insult to a copper
You can get two years.

Honor, lads, our brave policemen,
Even though it pains!
Tailors draw their pay in birch rods;
Cobblers theirs in canes.

Listen, good folks, to the warning
In this tale of woe:
When policemen come to fetch him,
Even God must go.

229

Už ho vedou svázaného,
všechno ve mně hrká!
Dva ho táhnou za ramena,
jeden vzadu strká.

HRKAT : RATTLE

STRKAT : PUSH

„Jenom mne po humnech ved'te,
však já s vámi pudu,
nedělejte mi ve městě
veřejnou ostudu!"

HUMNA : village
mje BACKYARD

VEŘEJNÝ : public
OSTUDA : shame

ZAPÍRAT :

Ale na humnech u strouhy
paní Perunice
zapírala Peruňátku
něco na sukničce.

STROUHA : ditch

Jak poznala svého pána,
hned se s hrozným křikem
na pochopy obořila
mokrým lavičníkem.

mi KŘIK : SHOUT
OBOŘIT : attack
LAVICE : bench
LAVIČNIK ma
bench wiper

mi
POCHOP = BiŘIC
BAILIFF /CONSTABLE

Ale Perun dobrotisko
sám ji napomíná:
„Schovej, ženo, meč do pochvy
přišla má hodina!"—

NAPOMÍNAT : admonish
SCHOVAT : put away

POCHVA : SHEATH
VAGINA
MEČ mi SWORD

Policajti s Perunicí
na humnech se vadí:
u dvora se zákoníci
o Peruna radí.

DVORANA - Hall/court
i the matter of Perun

RADIT : advise

A již Perun upoutaný
v šatlavě nocuje:
juristům se z paragrafů
žádný nešikuje.

ŠATLAVA : JAIL

POUTAT : Hold

šikuje off

Nebot' ten, kdo zákony d'ál,
neměl ani zdání,
že cár vezme někdy boha
do vyšetřování.

ŽDÁNI a thought

VYŠETŘVAT
investigate

230

There they bring him bound and fettered,
'Tis a sight of fear!
Two men pull him by the shoulders,
A third brings up the rear.

"Lead me down the backyard alleys,
Then I'll come with you;
But don't take me through the city
In the public view!"

On their way beside a ditch they
Met up with his spouse,
Washing something off their infant's
Tiny skirt and blouse.

When she recognized her husband,
She didn't think to lag,
But addressed the bailiffs roughly
With her laundry bag.

But Perun, the tender-hearted,
Spoke to her this word:
"Wife, my hour has finally come now,
Sheathe your fearful sword!"

While Perun's wife with policemen
Squabbles on the road
Lawyers in the court hunt pretexts
To apply the code.

And Perun, bound and fettered,
Sits all night in jail.
Judges, at a loss to charge him,
Still refuse him bail.

Long ago Vladimir's grandsire
Never thought to say
That a tsar might charge the Godhead
With lèse-majesté.

231

L. laesa majestos — injured majesty

Ráno přišla apelace
k cáru celá bledá,
že se proti Perunovi 3
zákon najít nedá.

Cár se na ně zle osopil,
řek jim, že jsou osli,
poslal hned pro vojenský soud
do kasáren posly.

Vojenský soud, to je samec,
soudí, jen se práši;
on má všechny paragrafy
v jedné patrontaši.

Vojenský soud na civilní
dívá se zvysoka,
nesoudí podle zákonů,
všechno jen od oka. 2

Vojenský soud má žaludek
zdravý jako štika:
2 nevinného na komando
stráví jak vinníka.

Vojenský soud z ničeho nic,
jako ňáký tvůrce,
nález právně potvrzený √
měl jako na šňůrce:

Že dle vyšlé proklamace
komandujícího
a dle ,,ostatních zákonů''
svodu hrdelního

4 pro urážku první třídy
? Jeho Veličenstvi,
pro vzpouru, nemravné řeči,
pro neposlušenství

232

Handwritten annotations:

apel : appeal
BLEDÝ : pale
OSOPIT : snap /rebuff
KASÁRNÍ BARRACKS
POSEL COURIER
SAMEC : male
strong
patrontaš
jen se práši
for all that time
?
jen : jenom
mfg / just
ŠTIKA : pike
STRÁVIT : digest
NEVINA : innocence
NEVINNÝ
POTVRDIT : ratify
NÁLEZ discovery
VINNÝ : guilty
TVŮRCE : creator
SŇŮRA : line immediately
dle : podle according to
OSTATNÍ the others
URÁŽKA : offense
VZPOURA : rebellion
MRAVNÍ : moral
HRDELNÍ of the throat
TŘÍDA : class
zákon law

All the judges wore pale aspects;
Vladimir was annoyed,
For the lawyers said the charges
Were quite null and void.

Straight away the tsar rebuked them,
Cursed their dull report,
Sent at once to army barracks
For a drumhead court.

Army courts are seldom partial
To a prisoner's cause:
In a cartridge case they carry
All they need of laws.

Army courts at civil judges
Look right down their nose;
How they reach judicial verdicts
Not e'en Heaven knows.

Army courts have stomachs ready
For all nourishment:
They digest both guilty culprits
And the innocent.

Army courts create from nothing,
Just as God once wrought,
Reaching verdicts clad in iron
Without a second thought.

This court-martial lost no time in
Handing down its sentence:
"Inasmuch as the indicted
Hasn't shown repentance,

"For high treason and sedition
And rebellion fiery,
And incriminating speeches
At the Court inquiry,

233

Křest
svatého
Vladimíra

Perun bůh jest odsouzený
k provazu dle práva,
že však k utopení v Dněpru
milost se mu dává;

bude ale pro výstrahu
neposlušné chase
vlečen k řece po ulicích
na konském ocase.—

Právě jeden žurnalista
seděl také v díře,
protože se bohu rouhal
a psal proti víře;

soud jej odsoudil, použiv
té příležitosti,
3   k stejnému trestu s Perunem
3   kvůli nestrannosti.—

Zpěv čtvrtý

TESTAMENT PERUNŮV

Poslyšte, milí křesťané,
tu smutnou novinu,
jak dokonal slovanský bůh
poslední hodinu.

Kdo máš tuze měkké srdce,
zacpi sobě uši
a pomodli se otčenáš
za ubohou duši.

Přivázali ho za nohy
na ocas kobyle,
blátem, kamením ho vlekli,
přežalostná chvíle!

234

"He, Perun, is hereby sentenced
In a noose to dangle,
But from mercy we will let him
Drown and not be strangled.

"As a warning to the young folk
(May it them avail!)
He'll be dragged down to the river
By a horse's tail."

There was then a poor reporter
In a nearby cell
Who had criticized religion,
Jeered at God as well.

To the same fate he was sentenced
By the same court-martial.
Thus the judges proved quite clearly
They could be impartial.

Canto IV

Perun's Testament

Listen, all you Christian people,
To this tale of gloom:
How the Slavic god encountered
His untimely doom.

If you have a heart too tender,
Stop your ears with tallow,
And three times repeat "Our Father"
For his soul unhallowed.

So they bound him by his ankles
To a mare's long tail,
Dragged him through the stones and puddles:
Oh what a mournful tale!

235

VALACH
Morvion shepherd
UKRUTNY - brutal
MUČIT - torture
LOUŽE - pool

KAT : executioner

lutriáni
vaj plund

VI NUK AT : suggest
VNUK
grandchild
SVIŇÁK
swine, shepherd.
KADIDLO - incense

KALUŽINA pool
puddle = louže
OBĚSIT : hang

Za ním toho novináře,
ouvej, ouvej, ach, ach,
šmejkal po břiše nelidsky
na ocase valach.

young
male horse

BŘICHO STOMA
NELIDSKY
in humar

Tak je ti cárští katané
ukrutně mučili,
všechny louže po Kyjově
s nimi vysmejčili.

Kiev

KATAN -killer

Když jsou je přivlekli k řece
celé plné bláta,
kati je tam utopili
jak slepá štěňata.

BLÁTO - mud

Umřeli jsou bez zpovědi
jako lutriáni,
jenom poslední jim dali
blátem pomazání.

confession

POMAZANÍ -
extreme unction

Já jsem sice při tom nebyl,
čet jsem to jen v plátku,
který o tom sepsal Nestor
vnukům na památku.—

plátek -
news paper.

„Tak to chodí na tom světě,
každou chvíli jinák:
dneska ctí tě za svatého,
zejtra budeš sviňák!

very
famous

Dnes vám, bozi, vy ubozí,
kadidlo lid pálí;
a zejtra vás jako smetí
v kalužinách válí.

smet' - speck

Dělají si nové bohy
dle svého pohodlí,
koho včerá oběsili,
k tomu se dnes modlí.

POHODLÍ com.

štěňě : puppy

After him the young reporter—
Alas, alas, alack!
To a gelding's tail they tied him,
Dragged him on his back.

Their tormentors cruelly prodded
The gelding and the mare,
Cleaned out all the Kiev puddles
With the luckless pair.

When they finally reached the Dnepr,
They were black with mud;
Like blind puppies there they drowned them
In the river's flood.

There they died without confession,
Just like Lutheran folk;
Mud served for their final unction—
'Twas a sorry joke.

It's quite true I wasn't there then;
I read it in the yearly
Which Friar Nestor left his children
Whom he loved so dearly.

"So it is in life, we know it,
Luck is often lacking:
Now they deem you ripe for sainthood,
Now they send you packing!

"Incense, O ye gods, they kindle,
In temples they now keep us;
But tomorrow things will alter:
In the streets they'll sweep us.

"New divinities replace us,
Made to suit man's whim:
Yesterday string up a scoundrel;
Today—all pray to him!

237

Křest
svatého
Vladimíra

Všechno jest na světě marné,
i království boží —
všechno hyne a pomine
jako špatné zboží.

Jenom cáři, samovláda
a takové sloty
potrvají věčně věkův
jak juchtové boty!"

Tak měl Perun, když ho vlekli,
rezonýrovati,
slyšel jsem to, a jak koupim,
musím prodávati.

238

"All in life is vain and foolish,
Even God's hereafter;
All that perishes and passes
Is only cause for laughter.

"Only tsars and autocrats
And such-like galoots
Last forever and forever,
Like stiff leather boots."

Thus Perun thought, as they dragged him,
So he meditated.
All this happened and was spoken
Just as I've related.

239

Křest
svatého
Vladimíra

Sám bych si to nevymyslil,
třeba bych to věděl,
dobře já vím, že bych za to
na Špimberku seděl.

Važ si všeho, milý synu,
co na trůnu sedí,
na ponížené dušinky
cár milostně hledí.

Kdo ctí cára a je Vávra,
může něčím býti,
kdo nechválí, bude věčně
jenom vodu píti.

240

I would never write inventions,
Even if I could:
Our police would string me up if
They misunderstood.

Honor all, my son, who govern
And sit on a throne:
Kings like subjects who obey them;
Make the others groan.

Fools can win success quite easily,
If they love their ruler;
If they don't, then all their lifetime
They'll sit in the cooler.

The baptism
of St.
Vladimir

*T*o the Czech revivalists all forms of folk art were of great interest as an expression of cultural nationalism: there were many who delved into folk lore and came up with songs and dances to which a quite false antiquity was ascribed. At the same time it became fashionable for poets to write in the folk style for a growing audience of Czech readers. The following song was published, and probably composed, by Arnost Forchgott-Tovacovsky (1835-74): but it has long been accepted into the repertoire of Czech folk art. Still sung today, it preserves the traditional symbolism of the rhythm of the seasons: amid the hard days of Czech history the promise of Spring is a hope for brighter days yet to come. The other song here included is found in variant versions in both Czech and Slovak: it may well be of Slovak origin, and adapted by Czech singers.

242

JARO

lidovělá

Přijde jaro, přijde,
zase bude máj,
usmívá se slunce,
usmívá se háj.
Stříbrné své vlny
hora vyleje,
rozkvete se růže,
slavík zapěje.

Rozpuknou se ledy,
volný bude proud,
po vlnách šumících
lodě pyšně plout;
vyskočí z hrud klasy
bujný bude květ,
kosa bude řinčet,
zpěv radostný znět.

A ta lípa naše
bude zelená,
z větví mocných listí
nám na věnce dá.
Ajta, vlasti, plesej.
Usmívá se háj,
přijde jaro, přijde,
budem míti máj.

THE SPRING

The Spring is coming, coming,
Once more it will be May,
Upon the smiling meadows
The smiling sun will play.
From mountain-side the river
Its silver waves will bring,
The rose will be in blossom,
The nightingale will sing.

The melting ice will scatter,
The current freely glide,
Upon the murmuring wavelets
The ships will proudly ride.
The flowers will richly blossom,
The ears spring from the ground,
The ringing scythe will echo,
A song of joy will sound.

The linden tree its branches
In greenness will array,
Its boughs will give us leafage
To make our garlands gay.
Then shout for joy, my country,
On fields the sun will play.
The Spring is coming, coming,
Once more we shall have May.

Traditional;
translated
by Alfred
French

243

MRTVÝ MILÝ

Zlidovělá

Když se Janko na vojnu bral,
tak své milé přikazoval:
Když nepřijdu za rok, za dva,
nečekej mě, milá, nikdá.

Po šest roků ho čekala,
na sedmý ho čarovala,
tak ho ona čarovala,
až se černá zem pukala.

Přijde Janko pod okénko,
potichoučku, polehounko.
Jak ho Hanka uviděla,
hned mu otevřít běžela.

Levou ruku mu podala
a pěkně ho privítala:
Vítej, vítej, Janko milý,
dávno jsme se neviděli.

Pober, Hanko, co je tvoje,
půjdeme my v širé pole,
v širé pole přeširoké,
pod to nebe pod vysoké.

244

THE DEAD LOVER

When Jan, the soldier, marched away
He told his sweetheart that fine day:
"Unless I come in two years' space
Then look no more to see my face!"

Six years went by; the seventh began:
She cast a spell upon her man.
She called, she called, her man away;
till the black earth yielded up its prey.

Jan came beneath her window sill;
Very silent; very still.
She saw him, and at once she ran,
To open up and greet her man.

She stretched her hand his hand to meet,
And very gently him did greet.
"O welcome, welcome, Jan, my dear;
I saw you not for many a year."

"Come Hannah, gather all you own,
Together to the fields we'll roam.
O come away to the fields with me
Below the heavens' canopy."

Traditional;
translated
by Alfred
French

245

A když ku hřbitovu došli,
na zelenou trávu sedli,
na zelenou trávu sedli,
a tak si tam povídali.

Ach Haničko, srdce moje,
pohledej mi v mojí hlavě,
ach Haničko, moje srdce,
povískej mi v mojí hlávce!

Kolik vlásků přehrnula,
tolik slzí uronila.
Ach Janíčku, srdce moje,
zetlelé jsou vlásky tvoje.

Jak by zetlelé nebyly,
vždyť šest roků v zemi hnily,
vždyť šest roků v zemi hnily
a na sedmý vstát musily.

And when they reached the cemetery,
They sat them down upon the lea.
They sat them down upon the lea
And talked together tenderly.

"O Hannah, dearest heart," he said,
"Come, look you closely on my head.
O Hannah, come, my lover fair,
O run your fingers through my hair!"

She smoothed his hair; she touched his head,
And many a piteous tear she shed.
"O Jan, O Jan, my lover true;
Your hair—your hair is rotted through!"

"How could it help but rot, my dear,
When in the earth it lies six year!
Six year it lies and rots away,
You brought it to the light of day."

247

25^{ho} Února

Sv. Matěj

Dnes je svatého Matěje:
kudy se hlas můj rozleje,
ať všude ovoce hojně je!
Pán Bůh rač nám dáti,
abychom měli co trhati:
jabka, hrušky, kadlátka,
ať je toho plná zahrádka.

Mikoláš Aleš

248

*I*n 1858 was launched the literary journal May, which became a platform for the ideas of a new wave of writers. The title was taken from Mácha's romantic poem, and the group consciously identified with the tradition he set; but in many ways the young writers were closer to the spirit of Havlíček. They followed a trend toward socially-committed literature, but avoided the romantic nationalism of their elders: the rustic idyll was now out of date, and the everyday world of city life became a popular subject for literary art.

The outstanding writer of the group, and possibly of the whole generation, was JAN NERUDA (1834-91), a journalist by profession. As the editor of a light magazine, Pictures of Life he helped to advance a whole literary programme, calling for an art based on the realities of Czech life, not on myths and dreams. Neruda's first collection of verse was Graveyard Flowers, whose main theme was the contrast between the busy, natural life of the surface, and the decay below—the restless ferment of social activity and the peace of the graveyard, which absorbs not only men's physical remains, but also their hopes and aspirations.

Neruda spent a lifetime writing for the popular press, and neither the monotony of his work nor the series of rebuffs he encountered succeeded in dampening his energy or his rebellious disposition. But with the passing years, his ideas changed, and he who began as an individualist and iconoclast, reserving his cruellist barbs for the patriotic pretentiousness of his elders, ended as an exponent of traditional folk art. In his collection Ballads and Romances, he returned, at the age of 49, to the themes of national tradition in a style so earthy and compact as to be worthy of the best folk poetry. As so often in the history of Czech literature, the rebel who expressed all the bitter frustration of the individualist in his youth, returned in the years of his maturity like a prodigal son to the service of the only collective whose discipline he acknowledged, that of his own folk and nation.

249

KAŽDÉHO JARA

Jan Neruda
(1834-1891)

Každého jara kmeny rév
přehorké slzy lijou,
že těch tak málo ve světě,
již jenom víno pijou.

Mně vše už jedno, zdali svět
teď stojí neb se točí,
jen nad osudem truchlých rév
zas pláčou moje oči.

ACH PRIŠLA LÁSKA

Ach přišla láska s milým žebroněním
a zaklepala stoudně na mé dvéře,
já vroucí dívku chladným okem měře
    ji hrubě odbyl: „Poděj!"

A přešla leta, s tklivým žebroněním,
svou všechnu náděj mdlým už okem měře,
jsem klepal sám na lásky bílé dvéře,
    a zvnitř to znělo: „Pozdě!"

250

EACH SPRING

Most bitter tears are shed each spring
By tendrils of the vine,
Because there are so few on earth
Who ne'er drink aught but wine.

It matters not to me if earth
Now twirls around or no,
Only the vine's sad fate again
Causes my tears to flow.

Translated
by Paul
Selver

LOVE CAME

Love came to me with tender supplication
And shamelessly sought entrance to my nook,
I gauged the maiden with a chilling look
    And gruffly mumbled: "Later."

The years passed by. With a mournful supplication
Measuring hopes with a weary, feeble look,
Alone I sought to enter love's white nook.
    A voice replied: "Too Late."

Translated
by R. A.
Ginsburg

251

ROMANCE O ČERNÉM JEZEŘE

Jan
Neruda

Tak tichá voda, hluboká a k smrti smutná!
Les kolem tichý, temný jako myrta rmutná,
břeh zadřímly a po něm mech jen roste hnědý,
a je-li v mechu květ, je jako z vosku bledý.
Zde nezní včelek šum, zde není zpěvný pták,
jen šedý dravec někdy v prázdné výši kráče,
a zní to v ozvěnách hor truchle tak,
jak v dáli náhlý škytot z dušeného pláče.

Můj zrak, sny opleten, se v černou vodu vrývá—
ta nezměřená tůň, ta něco dole skrývá.
Snad česká pohádka tam, z krajů vyhostěná.
Snad dávných bohů kruh tu kryje sklenná stěna.
Snad dlí tam českých našich hrdin slavný tem—
Vy bohorovní, úžasní Vy hrdinové,
již na Vás zapomněla sirá česká zem
a zapomnělo všechno pokolení nové!

Ti kdyby zaplakali pro národu hoře,
to černé jezero by vzrostlo v černé moře,
ti kdyby z živých prsou vzdechli, pozaštknuli,
svým vzdechem jezero by z břehů vymrsknuli!
Ach nekliden je asi pod vodami sen
a porván vzdechy těch, již spolu dole leží,
však jsou to umrlců již tiché vzdechy jen,
a povrchem to jako lehký mrazík běží.

THE BLACK LAKE

So silent lies the water, deep and deathly sad:
Around, the silent wood, like grieving myrtle dark,
The dreaming shore, and brown the moss that on it grows,
And any flower the moss reveals is pale as wax.
Here sounds no hum of bees, no singing bird is here,
Only, through empty skies, at times a bird of prey
Screams, and the echoing hills give back a sound as sad
As the sudden sob of muffled tears from far away.

My eyes, with dreams bemused, stare through the water
    black—
That pool unfathomed, what does it hide below?
Some old Bohemian legend, banished from the land?
Hides here that glassy wall some ring of ancient gods?
Rests here perhaps our great Bohemian hero band?
Noble and heroic, like the gods were you,
Forgotten by Bohemia's land forlorn,
Forgotten quite by all this generation new.

If they should weep for all their nation's grief,
Then that dark lake would swell into a darkling sea.
If they, from living breast, should sigh, their sobbing breath
Would send the lake in flooding deluge past its banks.
Below the water's edge, uneasy is the dream
And ruffled by the breath of them that lie below.
But now their breath is quiet—the breathing of the dead,
Across the lake like chilling breeze it seems to blow.

Translated
by Alfred
French

Snad podsvětí nás všech zde v podjezerním šeru.
Já zíral k horám kdysi v letním pološeru.
a zřel, že lesní strání, hlubnou v skalách slují
kés divné postavy jak voje sestupují.
Ne lidské podoby, jen proutky mlhy spíš
skrz kmeny tiskly se a s větve k větvi nesly,
než oko dostřehlo, již byly blíž a níž,
až jako šedý oblak na hladinu sklesly.

Ach smrt jich sílá denně od živoucích stolu,
že nestačí noc celá k podsvětí jim dolů,
a ranní hodiny když bílé světlo tkají,
ty zbylé stíny v lesy kol se utíkají.
Ba kdykoli jsem vstoup' v těch černých lesů lem,
hned divné šepoty jsem slýchal v krokův ruchu
a náhle v nepokojných tepnách cítil jsem,
že na mne z tmavých houštin zírá oko duchů.

Jen nahni se a zři ty hnědé rostlin nitě,
jak pod vodou se předou v pestře krásné sítě—
tam musí něco být, v té vodě nezčeřené,
a musí se cos krýt v té tůni nezměřené!
Jak lehký byl by skok, jak měkký dolů pád,
a člověk přistoup' by ku čárných bájů kolu—
já vím, já pevně dím: tam musí něco spát,
tam musí něco být—a mne to táhne dolů.

Perhaps our underworld is here, the dusk beneath the lake.
Through summer twilight once I gazed towards the hills
And saw, along the forest side, some figures strange
Like troops, descending to a cavern deep in rocks.
They seemed no human shapes but rather wisps of cloud,
Through trunks they moved, from branch to branch
*   among the brake,*
Before the eye could catch them, drawing near and low
And then, like greyish cloud, dissolving in the lake.

Each day death sends them forth, from living tables haled,
And night-time is too short for all to pass below.
But when the morning hours weave on the shining light,
The shades remaining turn and hurry to the woods.
Each time I stepped within the black woods' edge
Among the noise of steps I heard strange whispers fly,
And suddenly, with racing blood, I felt on me,
Gazing from gloomy copse, the stare of ghostly eye.

Bend down and gaze upon the trailing creepers brown
Below the water, see the lovely net they form—
Sure something must lie there, within that water calm,
And something must lie hid, within that massive pool.
How light would be that leap, how soft that fall below!
That ring of magic lore would open up its pit—
I know, I firmly hold, that something sleeps below—
For something must lie there, that draws me down to it.

ROMANCE O KARLU IV

Jan
Neruda

Král Karel s Buškem z Vilhartic
ted' zasedli si k dubovému stolu —
ti dva už pili mnohou číši spolu
a zapěli si z plných plic.
"Nuž dej sem zlaté číše, páže,
a nalej vína—dolej výš—
dnes, pane Bušku, čehos zvíš."
král Karel vesel káže.

"Zde po tom víně, Bušku, slyš,
domácí slunce naše vloni hrálo—
tot' první víno, které v Čechách zrálo—
aj tedy vzhůru, pijme již!"
A pili—král však náhle prsknul—
"To že je víno? tenhle kvas?
vždyt' křiví ústa, láme vaz."
a zlostně rukou mrsknul.

"Eh—vezu révu z Burgund sem,"
král dál a dál si v zlosti svojí vede,
"a takovouhle peluň mně z ní svede
ta velebená česká zem.
Jsem přesvědčen, když broskve vsadím,
že sčesám trpké trnky s nich,
a chceš-li klidit pustý smích,
zde růže sázet radím!"

"Však jaká země—taký lid!
vás kdyby učit chtěli všichni svatí,
zda všimnou si jich Češi paličatí—
bud' svatý rád, když není bit!
Jak bych zde mlátil otep slámy!
Necht' chci co chci, za krátký čas
se všechno jinak zvrtne zas—
mám já to bídu s vámi!"

256

THE BALLAD OF CHARLES IV

King Charles, with Bushek of Vilhart,
Sat down beside an oaken board.
Together many a cup they'd drunk
And many a hearty wassail roared.
"Come set out cups of gold, good page,"
In merry mood proclaims the king,
"And pour out wine—nay fuller yet,
Today, Bushek, thou'll see a thing."

"Hear me, Bushek, on these grapes
Last year our sun of home did shine.
Come, raise your glass and drink today
Of this, the first Bohemian wine."
They drank—the king in fury spat.
"I called it wine? This bitter froth!
This killing stuff! It twists the mouth."
And down he dashed his hand in wrath.

"I bring here vines from Burgundy,"
In rising anger spoke the king,
"And from Bohemia's noble land
I see such bitter wormwood spring.
For sure I'd tartest aloes reap
If I should sweetest peaches sow,
And here, if one would roses plant,
Hollow mockery would grow."

"Sure, but the folk are like the land.
If all the saints, to teach you, came,
(Should Czechs pay heed) be thankful, saints,
If blows at you they would not aim.
As well to thresh a sheaf of straw.
Try what I will—a day or two,
And all is turned about again.
Such rank return I have of you."

Translated
by Alfred
French

Přec zase číši k ústům zdvih',
a napiv se své velké dobré oči
ted' kradmo přes stůl po soudruhu točí,
ten však je jako pěna tich.
Jen—aby marně nezahálel—
pan Bušek máčel zub a pysk
a víno ku půnebí tisk'
a po jazyku válel.

"Ba je to bída" děl zas král
a rychle zavdal sobě vína znovu,
tak rychle, jak by bránil zlému slovu;
však kolem úst již úsměv hrál.
"Mám žízní umřít?—na mou víru,
Ty's oslep', páže—nevidíš,
že přede mnou je prázdná číš?—
a dej mi dobrou míru!"

"Pij, Bušku—již se nezarmut'—
a poslyš, co Ti král Tvůj moudrý praví:
můj jazyk je jak známo vybíravý—
a našel již v tom víně chut'.
Víš—zkoumat třeba, Bušku milý!
to víno má svůj zvláštní ráz,
zprv trpké, ale milé zas—
my, myslím, se už vpili."

"Nu vidíš, králi: tak náš lid!
Má duši zvláštní—trochu drsná zdá se—
však květe po svém, v osobité kráse—"
ted' přerušil svuj náhle klid
hned rozveselen Vilhartice—
"ach přibliž k tomu lidu hled
a přitiskneš svůj k němu ret
a neodtrhneš více."

Yet raised he to his lips the cup
And drank: his fine wide eyes now gave
A stealthy glance towards his friend:
Bushek sat silent as the grave.
And, but to find a thing to do,
He wet his lip the cup along
And to his palate pressed the wine,
And rolled it slowly round his tongue.

"Aye, wretched," said the king, and quick
He helped himself to wine the while,
So quick, as barring argument,
But round his lips now played a smile.
"Shall I then die of thirst? By heaven
Thou'rt blind, good page. Dost thou not see
An empty glass before me lies?
And let thy measure generous be!"

"Come, Bushek, drink. Be no more sad!
Thy king's wise words now savour.
My tongue discerning (as 'tis known)
Has found this wine's own flavour.
It hath its own peculiar charm,
One needs must try, dear Bushek, see—
First harsh perhaps, yet sweeter then,
Its taste by now is come to me."

"Why, see, my lord, just so our folk—
With temper strange and seeming rude—
Yet flowers in beauty all its own."
Vilhart, at once in merry mood,
Thus suddenly his silence broke.
"Look close upon that folk, I pray,
And thou to them wilt press thy lips,
Nor ever take thy lips away."

259

BALADA HORSKÁ

Jan
Neruda

"Řekněte mi, babičko má, co že rány svírá,

po čem člověk, těžce raněn, přece neumírá?" –

"Rány hojí otevřené na tom lidském těle

jenom čarodějná jarní šťáva z jitrocele." –

"Řekněte mi, babičko má, co se dobře dává,

je-li ochořelá hlava bolestí až žhavá?" –

"Na tak těžký úpal hlavy pomoc jiná není,

nežli mladé jarní listí z lesní jahodeni."

Dítě z chaty vyskočilo, do sousedních polí –

"Daruj šťávy, jitroceli, na vše co kde bolí."

S pole spěchá ku lesině, přes trní a hloží –

"Dej mi to své mladé listí, jahodino boží."

Co kde chtělo, rychle mělo, ke kostelu běží:

na kříži zde před oltářem Kristus rozpjat leží.

260

MOUNTAIN BALLAD

"Say what salve can close a wound
(Nanny, speak to me),
Heal and save from death a man
Wounded grievously?"

Translated
by Alfred
French

"To heal a mortal's open wounds
In a body ailing,
The spring juice of the plantain herb
Is alone availing."

"What is there can bring relief
(Nanny, speak to me),
When a head is hot with pain,
Throbbing ceaselessly?"

"To heal a head so feverish hot
Nothing else is good
Save the strawberry plant's young leaves,
Gathered in the wood."

From the cottage ran the child
Into the near-by field.
"Plantain herb, give me your juice,
That pain of man be healed."

From field to woods through thorns, through briars,
Onwards ran the child.
"Give me of your tender leaves,
Blessed strawberry wild."

She quickly gained what she had asked,
To church then sped away:
Jesus, stretched upon the cross,
Before the altar lay.

"Potírám Tvá svatá prsa, myju bok Tvůj svatý,

tělíčko zas uzdraví se, Ježíšku můj zlatý—

kladu čerstvé listí lesní na hlavu a líce,

nebude Ti hlavičku Tvou bodat úpal více!"

Nad kostelem velké zvony do vůkolí zvoní,

lid se sbíhá, v prsa bije, zázraku se kloní:

jak to dětská duše snila,

vůle boží vyplnila.

Podnes mají v horské vísce obraz Trpitele,

nemá rány ve svém boku, nemá trnu v čele,

bílá lilje v ranní záři po celičkém těle.

"See, I bathe Thy holy side,
Thy breast with ointment smear,
Thy dear wounds will heal again,
Jesu sweet, my dear.

Fresh leaves from the woods I lay
Upon Thy forehead sore,
The piercing fever's heart shall burn
Thy dear head no more."

The great bells on the church's top
Their summons loud are pealing.
The people gather, strike their breasts,
Before the wonder kneeling.
What her childish dream had willed
By the grace of God fulfilled.

That village still an image keeps
Of the Saviour born.
There are no wounds upon His side,
Upon His brow no thorn.
On all His body lilies white
Shining, as at dawn.

*A*DOLPH HEYDUK *(1835-1923) was an energetic member of the *May* literary group, and his early work illustrates their artistic programme. Familiar in his poems is the contrast between the poetic dream and the hard reality, between romantic patriotism and nationalist frustration. The gypsies of Slovakia appear in his work as symbolic victims of ethnic and social injustice; their rich Romanic lore, which Heyduk explored in his *Gypsy Songs*, contrast with hopeless and homeless poverty. Personal tragedy lent an added touch of gloom to his later work, which became more nostalgic in feeling, and marked by dalliance with melancholy resignation.*

265

DUMA V BOUŘI JARNÍ

Adolf Heyduk
(1835-1923)

Jarní bouře, jarní bouře,
hej, jak smetá sníh i prach;
luhy mladnou, lesy mladnou,
ledy tají na horách.

Jarní bouře, jarní bouře,
všecko jasno, čisto kol;
staré kmeny pučí znova,
z kypré země žene stvol.

Jarní bouře, jarní bouře,
co je shnilo, trhej, ruj! . .
Jarní bouře, jarní bouře,
kdy jí budeš, lide můj?

266

THOUGHTS ON A SPRING STORM

Springtime tempest, springtime tempest,
How you scatter dust and snow!
Field and forest stir and quicken;
Mountain ice-drifts melt and go.

Springtime tempest, springtime tempest,
Earth grows spotless in your train;
Trunks once bare now bud in beauty;
From the furrows springs the grain.

Springtime tempest, how you vanquish
All that rots and putrefies!
As a cleansing springtime tempest
When, my folk, wilt thou arise?

Translated
by Watson
Kirkconnell

267

*A*nother prominent member of the May group was *VÍTĚZ-SLAV HÁLEK (1835-1874)* who in his lifetime was regarded as the most successful writer of the day. Poet, dramatist, journalist, critic and cultural organizer, Hálek achieved prominence in almost all sections of literary life, and left a large body of work. More naive and optimistic in his policies than was his friend and collaborator Neruda, he excelled him in popularity: but his elevated—consciously poetic—style, and his idealistic views on art, have rather dated his work. Perhaps he will be longest remembered as a poet of nature.

269

UMLKLO STROMŮ ŠUMĚNÍ

Vítězslav
Hálek

Umlklo stromů šumění
a lístek sotva dýše,
a ptáček dřímá krásný sen
tak tichounce, tak tiše.

Na nebi vzešlo mnoho hvězd
a kolem je tak volno,
jenom v těch ňadrech teskno tak
a v srdci tak bolno.

Ve kvítků pěkný kalíšek
se bílá rosa skládá,
můj Bože, a ta rosa též
se v moje oči vkrádá.

270

THE RUSTLE OF THE TREES IS HUSHED

The rustle of the trees is hushed,
The leaves hang breathlessly,
A bird dreams on in tranquil sleep,
So still, so noiselessly.

Many stars have climbed the sky,
Around them emptiness.
A desolation in the breast,
At heart a loneliness.

Within the chalice of the flowers
The dewy crystals rise.
O God, I feel the drops of dew
Come stealing to my eyes.

Translated
by Alfred
French

*I*n the history of Czech literature there have been several swings of fashion between nationalism and cosmopolitanism—between the adherents of the folk tradition and those who sought to throw open the windows of Bohemia to foreign air, and consciously tried to catch up with modern trends abroad. In 1863 was founded the Arts Group (*Umělecká Beseda*) in Prague, which gathered round it a brilliant collection of writers and artists. By its sponsorship of concerts, lectures, and exhibitions of Czech and foreign work it did much to encourage an international artistic atmosphere in the capital. On the other hand Czech nationalism was proving a powerful influence in public life and in art. In 1861 the first Czech political newspaper was launched; in 1863 Smetana produced his opera *The Bartered Bride;* in 1868 was laid the foundation stone of the *Czech theatre.*

The younger literary generation rode the tide of national fervour. Like the Romantics before them they sought virtue in the tradition of Czech folk art and history, but their approach, based on ideological conviction, was intellectual rather than naive, and their style tended toward a rhetoric which eventually dampened its appeal. The outstanding poet of the group was *SVATOPLUK CĚCH (1846-1908),* who celebrated patriotic, historical, and Slavic themes in a series of verse epics and allegories. He is perhaps best remembered for his collection *Pisně otroka (Songs of a Slave)* published towards the end of his life, and obliquely expressing the Czech national problem. Modern readers may find his work most attractive where the rhetoric is muted, and the social commitment less overt, as in the following, almost Burnsian, lyrics.

273

JAK JITŘNÍM POUPĚTI

Svatopluk
Čech
(1846-1908)

Jak jitřním poupěti
plá krůpěj rosy,
jak prsten v objetí
svou perlu nosí,
jak nebe hvězdy jas
a křišťál horská sluj:
tak chová v každý čas
mé srdce obraz tvůj.

Spíš v dol se pohoří,
v souš moře změní,
spíš slunce dohoří
a luny skvění,
spíš ve mně živoucí
bít srdce ustane,
než k tobě horoucí
v něm láska doplane.

AT DAWN

As when a dewy crystal
A bud displays at dawn,
As when a single jewel
Upon a ring is borne,
As when the sky the starlight,
A cave a crystal holds,
So too my heart your portrait
For ever more enfolds.

The hills will change to valleys
The ocean will run dry,
The sun will shine no longer
The gleaming moonlight die;
The heart will cease its beating
Within my living breast,
Before my love that blazes
For you, will sink to rest.

Translated
by Alfred
French

NA ŠIROKÝCH POLÍCH

Svatopluk
Čech

Na širokých polích,
na dalekých polích,
jaká krása dnes!
Stébel husté davy
výše mužské hlavy
stojí jako les.

Klasů jasné vlny
těžkým zrním plny
šumí vedle cest,
a když van je sehne,
mezi nimi šlehne
na sta modrých hvězd.

V brokátovém hávě,
v plné letní slávě
září každý lán,
těší se své kráse,
všecek usmívá se,
sluncem zulíbán.

Však tu nivou náhle
prochvělo cos táhle
jako teskný vzdech,
jak by všechno zbledlo,
s uleknutím vzhledlo
k hrstce šedých střech.

Odtud blesklo cosi—
zasvitly tam kosy
v jitřním pablesku,
s nimi na rameně
muži odměřeně
vyšli na stezku.

UPON THE ROLLING FIELDS

Upon the rolling fields
Upon the distant fields
Today, what beauty lies!
The stalks in massed array
As high as human head
A spreading forest rise.

They rustle by the paths
As heavy grain weighs down
The shining waves of corn;
Then as they bow in wind
Among the stalks like stars
A flash of blue is born.

In glittering brocade
Each shining meadow gleams,
In summer glory dressed;
All smiling in its joy
To feel its loveliness
By sunny lips caressed.

Then like a frightened gasp,
Abruptly through the plain
A rippling shudder ran;
As if the fields grew pale
And turned in sudden fear
The clustering roofs to scan.

From there a light had flashed,
The glint of scythes that pierced
The dim-lit morning haze;
The scythes that shoulders bore
Of men that paced along
Towards the trodden ways.

Translated
by Alfred
French

Postavy to silné;
ruce tvrdé, žilné;
osmahlá je plet';
i hrud', zpráhlá žárem,
režných košil spárem
svítí jako měd'.

Sbor ten, s krbci v pasu,
došel k moři klasů,
kosy sklonil v zem,
nahoře pak na ně
složil drsné dlaně,
chvíli postál něm.

Ještě v zadumání
rozhlíží se plání
přes ten zlatý les,
pnoucí se tu v pýše
po široké líše
naposledy dnes.

278

Powerful, sunburnt men
Whose thick and hardened arms
The veins stood out upon;
Between the home-spun shirt
Each weather-beaten chest
Like burnished copper shone.

They came, with pouch on hip,
And laid their scythes to ground
Beside that waving sea;
Then on the handle set
Their hardened palms and stood
A moment silently.

Still thoughtfully they gazed
Where sweeping through the plains
That golden forest lay;
Across the broad expanse
Exulting in its pride
On this, its final day.

Upon the
rolling
fields

The feeling of dedication to a national or social cause may give writers a feeling of confidence in themselves, and in the vital importance of art. On the other hand nationalist and ideological preoccupations serve to date literature, and, by narrowing its horizons, eventually to clip its wings. Where this happens, a new generation of writers sees its function in righting the balance, in swinging from national to international criteria and from a literature ideologically motivated to one recognising no authority above itself. During the 1870's a group of Czech writers, grouped around the journal Lumir, became known for a programme which was openly cosmopolitan, and which sought to break the restrictive influences of national, social and political pressure. They are often known as Parnassians, after the French school of poets, and their most distinguished representatives were J. Vrchlický, J. V. Sládek and J. Zeyer. They were gifted translators; Sládek is perhaps best known for his translations from English poetry, while Vrchlický included in his enormous literary output translation from the classics, from Romance languages, and from German, and Polish.

Although JAROSLAV VRCHLICKÝ (1853-1912) in his work reacted against the tendency to narrow the horizons of literature, it would be an error to identify him with the exponents of art for its own sake. In his Legend of St. Prokop he celebrated a hero of Czech myth, and revealed a nationalism no less fervent than that of his contemporary, Svatopluk Čech. But it was the culture of the past, especially that of Greek and Roman classical art, which exerted the greatest influence on Vrchlický's verse: he has been described in a paradoxical anachronism as the first Czech poet of the Renaissance. Not only did he translate from Greek and Latin poetry with much erudition and grace, but by his introduction of classical metres and motifs into Czech he increased the literary capital of future poets.

Vrchlický has been likened to the poet Swinburn, and his poetry described by admirers as learned, rich, brilliant, and monumental—adjectives which themselves may contain overtones of scepticism. The immense quantity of his output is rather daunting, and there is undoubtedly a good deal in his published work which seems tired and hackneyed.

281

ADAGIO

Jaroslav
Vrchlický
(1853-1912)

Do velké, šedé škeble mramoru,
kde místo vody svadlé listí leží,
se kloní větve bříz a javorů.
Vše v dřímotě, jen mraky nebem běží.
Zde chtěl bych státi v zamyšlení dumném
a dívat se, jak večer táhne sem,
a luňák v letu posupném a šumném
jak po kořisti slídí nad lesem;
tou sochou chtěl bych býti kamennou,
jež o samotě dumá v lesní hloubi,
jež s větry mluví jen a ozvěnou,
na jejíž skráni s nocí den se snoubí.

ADAGIO

Over the marble with its great drab shell, Translated by Paul Selver
Where faded leaves in place of water lie,
The boughs of birches and of maples fell:
All slumbers, save the scudding clouds on high.
Fain would I linger here in wistful poring,
And gaze at evening drawing nigh this way;
And at the hawk's gloom-covered, clamorous soaring,
How o'er the wood he watches for his prey;
Fain would I be this statue wrought in stone,
On loneliness in forest-depths to brood,
Speaking with winds and echo all alone,
Upon whose brow the night by day is wooed.

VÁNOCE

Jaroslav
Vrchlický

Hlas zvonů táhne nad závějí,
kdes v dálce tiše zaniká;
dnes všechny struny v srdci znějí,
neb mladost se jich dotýká.

Jak strom jen pohne haluzemi,
hned střásá ledné křišťály,
rampouchy se střech visí k zemi
jak varhan velké píšťaly.

Zem jak by liliemi zkvetla,
kam sníh pad, tam se zachytil;
Bůh úsměv v tvářích, v oknech světla
a v nebi hvězdy rozsvítil.

A staré písně v duši znějí
a s nimi jdou sny jesliček
kol hlavy mé, jak ve závěji
hlas tratících se rolniček.

Můj duch zas tone v blaha moři,
vzdech srdcem táhne hluboce,
a zvony znějí, světla hoří—
Ó vánoce! Ó vánoce!

284

CHRISTMAS

Above the snow drift, sound of bells
Is fading into distant space.
The strings of every heart are singing
Touched, this day, with youthful grace.

Translated
by Alfred
French

Each movement of the branches sees
A crystal shower of ice descend.
From roof to ground the icicles
Like massive organ pipes extend.

As if the earth with lilies bloomed,
The fallen snowflakes freezing lie.
God lights up smiles—and window panes—
And starlight shining in the sky.

Old songs are sounding in my heart,
As dreams to Bethlehem are winging.
Round my head, as in a snow drift,
Dying sound of sleigh bells ringing.

Sighing deep, I feel my heart
Once more through seas of rapture glide.
And bells are sounding, lights are burning.
Christmas tide! Oh Christmas tide!

285

MARCO POLO

Jaroslav
Vrchlický

Já Marco Polo, Benátčan a křesťan,
vyznávám Boha v Trojici a doufám
na věčnou spásu hříšné svojí duše.
To víra má i naděj. Co má láska,
vy ptáte se? Já klidně odpovídám:
Mou láskou veliké jsou dálné cesty,
vždy nové obzory, vždy noví lidé
a nová dobrodružství mořem, souší
a nové obchody. (To krev mých dědů.)
Já mnoho viděl, o mnohém jsem slyšel,
v kraj přišel, o němž se vám sotva zdálo,
kde roste jantar jako zlaté proutí,
kde salamandra (vámi zvaná asbest)
jak zkamenělé lilje plá a kvete,
kde žhoucí nafta z vnitra země teče,
kde rubínů jest řeřabin jak v zimě,
kde lopatky a záda tetovují
si orla s obrazem, kde pouze ženy
jen vládnou, muži kde jsou k tuhým službám
po porodech žen dáni na vymření.

Já viděl chána Kytajského říši,
jed' s lidojedy u jednoho stolu,
byl vlnou v příboji a velký smaragd
(pro vezíra byl určen Bagdadského)
jsem prones' celou pouští pod jazykem.

286

MARCO POLO

I, MARCO POLO, Christian and Venetian,
Acknowledge God the Trinity and cherish
Hope of salvation in eternity
For my sin-laden soul: in this my faith,
In this my trust is set. What of my love,
Ye ask? And I give answer tranquilly:
My love is long and distant journeys; ever
New-found horizons, new-found peoples, fresh
Exploits on ocean and dry land, and ever
Fresh enterprises. (This, my forebears' blood)
Much have I seen, to much have given ear;
I reached the land, whereof ye scarce have inkling,
Where amber grows like golden foliage,
Where salamanders (that ye dub asbestos)
Blossom and blaze like lilies petrified,
Where glowing naphtha gushes from the earth,
Where there is equal wealth of rubies, as
Of holly here in winter; where across
Their back and on their shoulders they tattoo
The image of an eagle; where the women
Alone rule, and the men are given up
From birth to heavy service till they die.
I gazed upon the realm whose ruler is
Khan of Cathay; and I have sat at meat
With those who feed on men: I was as a wave
Amid the surf: the mighty emerald
(Pre-destined for the vizier of Bagdad)
Beneath my tongue I carried through the desert.

Translated
by Paul
Selver

Marco
Polo

Se sedla třicet dnů a třicet nocí
jsem nesestoup'. Já viděl velké pouště
se v dálku vlnit zcuchané jak roucho,
spát moře v měsíci jak tuhý rubáš,
plát hvězdy cizí cizích zeměpásů.
Já navštívil jsem říši kněze Jana,
kde dobro, ctnost a spravedlnost vládly
jak v pohádce, ba skoro ted' mi zdá se,
že přišel jsem i v podivný kout země,
kde zastavil se druhdy Alexandr
na pouti indické, kdy nemoh' dále
pro valné deště, které neustaly.
(Snad říše vil v tom dotknul se, snad města
již božího a couvnul hrůzou zpátky,
když z brány anděl na své dlani lebku
mu podával, řka: ,,Takou tvoje bude
za roků pár a víc nebude vážit!'')
Já viděl i tu zemi tajuplnou,
kde zemský ráj byl, kde zdroj mládí teče
v tisíci jiných ukryt mezi travou,
já z mnohých pil, dost možná, že i z mládí,
a proto všecko vydržel jsem s chutí,
a proto všecko jako ve zrcadle
zřím v duši své a dnes to mohu popsat.
Svět změní tvář svou. Umru jako jiní,
však moje dědictví, to zbude světu:
Ta choutka dál, vše viděti a poznat,
vše vykořistit ku člověka blahu.
Mých synů bude legie, dál půjdou,
než moh' jsem já, však sotva uzří více,
neb z divů svléká svět se jak had z kůže.
Já znám tu starou plnou snů a tajů,
a to mi stačí. Ti, kdo za mnou přijdou,
at' pomohou si, jak to právě půjde,
jak pomoh' já si, dál at' za vděk vezmou,
co zbude jim. U večeře cest dlouhých
já sedím první, výtečně mi chutná,
vše jde mi k duhu a vše dobře strávím.

For thirty days and nights I came not down
Out of my saddle. I have seen great deserts
Like ruffled raiment billowing afar;
The ocean sleeping underneath the moon
Like a stiff winding-sheet; strange stars ablaze
Beneath strange zones. I visited the realms
Of Prester John, where goodness, virtue and
Righteousness ruled, as in a legend, —yea,
Now meseems almost that I even reached
The wondrous nook of earth, where Alexander
Once lighted on the wilderness of Ind,
And came no farther on his way, because
Of mighty downpours that abated not.
(Perchance upon the faery realm he there
Set foot, or e'en upon the town celestial,
And shrank away in dread, when at the gate
An angel put a skull into his hand,
Saying' "A few more years, and this shall be
Thy portion, —this, and not a tittle more!")
And I beheld that land of mystery
Where lay the paradise of earth, where flowed
The spring of youth, concealed within the grass
Amid a thousand others, whence I drank
From many, and, 'tis very like, from youth:
And therefore all endured I with acclaim,
And therefore all, as in a mirror, I
Perceive within my soul, and now portray it.
The world is changed of aspect: I shall die
Like others, but my heritage remains:
The lust for seeing all and learning all,
To ransack all for the delight of man;
Legion shall be my sons: they shall proceed
Farther than I, but scarcely shall see more,
For earth sheds wonders as a snake its skin.
Old age I know, with many dreams and secrets
And that suffices me. And they who come
After me, let them take, as it may chance,
Of what remains to them, as best they can,
As I did. I sit foremost at the feast
Of distant journeys, and it likes me well.
All prospers me, and I fare well with all.

Nad knihami své celé probdít žití,
se hádat v žlutých pergamenů směsi
o písmena, o smysl, hledat pravdu,
je mnoho ovšem; v táborech věk prožít
při vřesku trub a polnic ve útocích,
nad valy v dešti střel, v měst rozvalinách,
v žen nářku, dětí pláči, vzlyku padlých,
je mnoho ovšem; býti svatý biskup
a vésti k nebi legiony duší,
(jichž ani nezná), pouhé víry těchou
a slovem božím, v mramoru a zlatě
jen žalmů slyšet spád a snivý smutek,
je mnoho ovšem; vidět však a znáti
na vlastní oči dálné, širé země
a moře, pláně a zhvězdění nebes
a různý lid, mrav jeho, zvyky, bohy,
též něco platí a má zvláštní půvab
novinky věčné. A já jsem to zažil,
já Marko Polo, Benátčan a křesťan.

To make all life a vigil over books,
To rack one's brain 'mid piles of yellow parchments
Seeking the truth of writing and of thought,
Is much, in sooth; to live an age in camps
'Mid roll of drums and trumpets in assaults,
O'er ramparts in a rain of missiles, in
Ruins of towns, amid laments of women,
Weeping of children, groaning of the fallen,
Is much, in sooth; to be a holy bishop,
Legions of spirits to escort to heaven,
(The which he knoweth not) by solace of
The faith alone, and by the word of God,
In marble and in gold to hearken to
The cadence and the dreamy grief of psalms,
Is much, in sooth; but to behold and know
With one's own eyes the distant, ample lands,
And oceans, plains and star-tracks of the skies,
And divers folk, their habit, usage, gods,
This too, availeth something, and hath charm
By special token of its newness, that
Doth ever change. And I have savoured this,
I, Marco Polo, Christian and Venetian.

At an early age JOSEF VÁCLAV SLÁDEK (1845-1912) turned from a study of science to creative literature; a stay overseas in America added to his worldly experience and had lasting effects on his literary interests. After returning to Prague as a university teacher of English, he achieved distinction by his translations from Longfellow, Bret Harte, Byron, and, above all, from Shakespeare. For more than twenty years he edited the journal Lumír, and by his example he helped to lead a literary generation still plagued with provincialism towards a more cosmopolitan style. Sládek is at his best as a poet of short personal lyrics: the love verses, and intimate elegies for which he is well known, have an unusually personal ring—frequently recalling the poet's romantic nostalgia for the sea, and the tragedy of his young wife's death. A mark of his culture is a restraint which saves him from contemporary sentimentality, and a simplicity which often gives his poems an air of folk songs or children's verses. Sládek was in fact one of the first Czech poets to write specifically for children, and his work in this regard was to be fruitful for later literature.

SEN

Josef
Václav
Sládek
(1845-1912)

Mně o kouzelné zahrádce
　se zdál tak divný sen,
to bylo jako v pohádce,
　když v soumrak přejde den.

V měsíčném svitu s jabloně
　květ po květu se chvěl,
a v porosèném záhoně
　se černý motýl tměl.

A kol jak stromy šelestí,
　pták zlatý zpíval tam.
„To zpívá píseň o štěstí,"
　já pravil k sobě sám.

Tu vráz, jak na vše pad by strach,
　pták zachvěl se a ztich:
Pochmurný stín mu k srdci sáh
　a na vše napad sníh.

294

A DREAM

I dreamed of an enchanted garden—
the strange and haunted sight
of a fairytale landscape, pictured
in the fading evening light.

Translated
by Alfred
French

An apple tree stood in the moonlight;
massed flowers across the sky:
on the dew-decked garden there fluttered
a black-winged butterfly.

The rustling branches were moving,
by a warbler's melody stirred;
and I thought: 'A song of pure rapture!'
at the voice of the golden bird.

All at once—like a blanket of terror—
the bird stopped in the midst of his sound.
On his heart fell a sinister shadow;
and the snow fell all around.

TRÁVA

Josef
Václav
Sládek

Za moře jsi neodešla,
    nejsi ani za horami,
jen ta hrstka polní trávy
    roste, roste mezi námi.

Za ty hory ptáče letí,
    přes to moře vítr táhne,
ale zde, tou hrstkou trávy,
    ruka ruky nedosáhne.

GRASS

Dividing us there lies no sea,
nor mountain barrier:
only a handful of spreading grass
is our growing frontier.

A bird flies over the mountain tops,
and the wind sweeps over the sea,
but that little grass holds our searching hands
apart eternally.

Translated
by Alfred
French

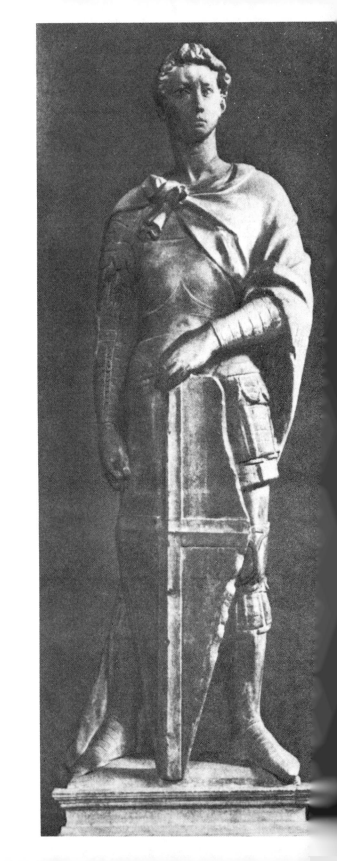

In the whole field of XIXth century Czech literature there can be few writers of more cultivated and cosmopolitan taste than JULIUS ZEYER (1841-1901). His commitment to Czech literature was in contrast to the Franco-German cultural background of his parents; and his devotion to a career of creative writing was in spite of a technical education designed to fit him to take over a family business. Zeyer travelled widely in Western and Southern Europe, and spent several periods in Russia, where he worked as tutor. Coming late to an Arts course, he studied Classics at the Caroline University in Prague, and visited Greece and Turkey at a time when it was unusual for West European Classical scholars to travel as far as Rome, let alone to Athens. In Zeyer's work, motifs familiar in Czech folk and literary tradition mingle happily with those from his rich intellectual background. He wrote drama, and novels tinged with cultivated irony; but it is by his verse that he is most likely to be remembered. A gifted lyric poet, he experimented with epic forms, using material drawn from Czech and foreign legend. A Romantic in his attitudes and choice of themes, he avoids the danger of sentimentality by the exercise of that restraint which is the mark of his culture. Zeyer has been described as a Czech pre-raphaelite, and his narrative verse compared to that of William Morris. It is here perhaps that Czech verse approaches most closely in spirit that of English poetry of the XIXth century.

299

POUŤ

Julius
Zeyer
(1841-1901)

Pout'dokonána. Zase na sever
zpět vrátil jsem se z končin slunnějších:
ty leží nyní za mnou daleko
jak moje mládí. Avšak neteskním,
vždyt'plna vzpomínek je duše má
jak na světlý ten jih, tak na jasnou
tu nivu mladosti. Nuž, neteskním.
Hůl poutnickou jsem tiše postavil
v kout síně své a s něhou shledání
na luka hledím, lesy, na vody,
v tvář dávné této vlasti, po které
vždy v dáli toužím. Věru, zdá se mi,
že zrak mi vlhne, nebot' tušení,
že doba blízká, kdy se rozloučím
s tím krajem navždy, jenž mi drahým byl,
se ve mně ozývá jak vzdálený
zvuk zvonu, který mlhou večerní
se nese tesklivě. Já půjdu tam,
kam všechna pokolení odešla,
a lesy budou dále v slunci snít
a vody dřímat v lesku bílých hvězd . . .

PILGRIMAGE

My pilgrim's staff I have quietly laid by
In a corner of my room. With tenderness
I gaze once more on forest, field and stream,
The features of that immemorial face
For which I longed in absence. O, my country!
My eyes grow dim with the foreboding thought
Of the approaching time, when I must take
My last farewell of this beloved land.
Distant and dread there echoes in my ear
The beat of a bell, that through the evening mist
Tolls sombrely. I am going to that place
Where all past generations wait for me,
And still the sun will gild these dreaming woods,
These water slumber under the white stars—

Translated
by E.
Pargeter

Z JARA

Julius
Zeyer

Drozd zpívá už v háji,
ó zlatý zvuk,
pln touhy a něhy,
pln sladkých muk!

Jak smavá je niva,
zelený lán,
co šeptá jim tajů
ten větrů van!

A skřivan ted' v bouři
svou píseň vznes'
jak pějící hvězda
nad temný les.

Je slunce, je jaro,
je zlatý máj,
zas vrátila dávná
se snivá báj.

Ó jaro, ó máji,
jaký to ruch,
jak zmlazena země,
jak siný vzduch!

Jak všude je světlo,
jak blaze kol—
jen v srdci mém smutek
a stesk a bol.

Má láska bez lásky
tam krvácí,
a v hrob ten se máj můj
už nevrací!

302

TO SPRING

The thrushes throng the grove—
O golden notes,
Drenched with desire and love
From fairy throats!

Translated
by Watson
Kirkconnell

How jocund are the field
And meadow greening!
What whisper has revealed
The warm wind's meaning?

A lark aloft outfloods
His chant afar,
As above sombre woods
A courier star.

The sun, the spring are here
And May's green dance.
The dreaming days appear
Of old romance.

Ah spring, ah May, in sooth
How throbs this hour!
How earth renews her youth!
The air, her power!

How everywhere lie light
And happiness! —
But in my heart the blight
Of grief's distress.

There sad love sorrowing
Bleeds slow away;
For in the grave my spring
Is laid for aye.

LEGENDA O DONATELLOVI

Julius
Zeyer

Po celé Florencii vzruch a šum,
neb skončil Donatello sochu svou.
pod baldachýnem z krajek kamenných,
jenž bílý oblouk v blankyt směle pne
hle, stojí svatý Jiří se štítem,
ten symbol Florentinské volnosti,
ta socha velebná v své prostotě,
již Donatello věčný život vdech',
již za duši dal vlastní duše vzlet,
již do čela byl vepsal rekovnost ...

Po celý den se tlačí lidu dav
a plesá před zářícím mramorem
a jméno Donatello městem zní
jak hudba, jako píseň vítězná;
tak naplněn jest jeho chválou vzduch,
že výkřiky a slova nadšení
až do příbytku mistra vnikají.

Tam, v stínu dílny, bled a zamyšlen
se halí Donatello v tmavý plášť',
jak by jej mrazil planý slávy ryk.
jest mučedníkem každý umělec,
neb v srdci jeho tajném úkrytě
červ pochybnosti hlodá napořád;
jen tenkráte, když hana závistná
plod jeho ducha jedem potřísní,
jen tenkráte umlkne pochybnost,
by ustoupila vzdoru hrdému.
Pak vzplane oko, cuká bledá tvář,
a tichý umělec se vrhá v boj
jak tygřice se řítí na vraha,
jenž mláďata jí hrozí usmrtit.
Ó, jeho bol jest krutší jejího,
vždyť' tygřice jen mlékem kojila,
však umělec krev svého srdce dal! ...

304

DONATELLO, A LEGEND

All Florence is astir with hum and haste,
For Donatello's statue is complete.
Beneath a canopy of stony lace
That towards the sky projects its daring arch,
Behold! St. George stands with his polished shield,
The symbol of Florentian liberty;
That statue of sublime simplicity
To whom its maker gave eternal life,
To whom he gave his soul's unfettered flight,
Upon whose brow he wrote heroic deeds.

Translated
by R. A.
Ginsburg

All through the day, the people mill about,
Rejoicing round the gleaming, marble form.
Young Donatello's name resounds throughout the town
Like music or a trimphant battle song.
The air is so suffused with all this praise,
That the shouts and words of unrestrained delight
Reach high into the sculptor's darkened room.

There, pale and musing, in his shaded nook,
Sits Donatello, wrapped in gloomy cloak,
As if such hollow fame had chilled him through.
Yest, every artist suffers martyrdom;
For in the secret places of his heart
The worm of doubt relentlessly gnaws on:
And only when the slurs of envy born
Spatter with venom the products of his soul,
The artist stills these gnawing, prying doubts
To let defiance take their place.
Then with a sparkling eye and twitching, pallid cheeks
The quiet artist plunges in the fray
Like a tigress leaping at an enemy
That stalks to slay her unsuspecting young.
His suffering exceeds the tigress' pains,
For she gives only milk to feed her young,
But the artist gives the life blood from his heart!

305

Tak tráví Donatello v myšlenkách
ten celý dlouhý, slunnojasný den,
a když na večer ztichly ulice
a snivé noci hvězdná nádhera
nad městem v plné kráse vzplanula,
tu dvéře svého domu otevřel,
a zastaviv své kroky na prahu,
tak Donatello mluví v srdci svém:
„Čím chvála, čím mi hana davu jest?
Jen vánkem, který vzniká, zaniká
a stopy nezanechá za sebou . . .
Však hlavu svoji skláním hluboce
před mistra svého soudným výrokem,
vždyť jeho ret jest svaté pravdy stan,
a duše jeho věčné krásy chrám!
Nechť spravedlivě skráň mi ověnčí—
laur vínkem mojím buď, či ostrý hloh!"
Jde Donatello krokem zrychleným
a najde svého mistra bdícího
na střeše domu, odkud vidět jest
na spící město, řeku šumivou,
na ztmělé stromy zahrad vonících,
kde v trávě bloudí žhavé světlušky,
na modrý věnec dálných Apenin,
nad jejichž výší plavá luna sní.

„Můj mistře," zvolá, „drahý mistře můj!"
Tu zraky kmeta, plny paprsků,
jež z kmitajících nebes v duši vssál,
se obrací na učně bledou tvář:
„Já na tě čekal, Donatello můj!"
A Donatello ruku uchopí,
již na pozdrav mu mistr podává,
a hlasem, chvějícím se pohnutím,
tak z hloubi vřelé duše promluví:
„Můj otče, ó můj pane vznešený,
jenž moje kroky řídil's nesmělé
po oné dráze plné kamení,
co vzhůru vede k výši závratné —
ó, odpověz při spáse duše své! . . .

Thus Donatello spends in prying thoughts
The slowly passing, drawn-out, sunlit day.
And when at length the streets at dusk are stilled,
And the starry splendor of the dreamy night
Blazes in glory on the sleeping town,
Then Donatello slowly steps abroad,
And pausing on the threshold of his home,
Thus muses in his aching, burdened heart.
"What means the peoples' praise and blame to me?
A shifting wind that comes and goes at will
And leaves no trace behind once it is gone.
But humbly, deeply I will bow my head
Before my master's most judicious words,
Because his lips are like a tent of truth,
His soul a shrine of all that is beautiful.
Upon my temples he alone shall place
A laurel wreath, or else a hawthorn leaf."
Then with a quickened step he hastens forth
And finds his aged master still awake,
Upon a roof from whence the aged eyes can see
The sleeping city and the whispering stream;
The scented garden's darkened leafy trees
Where blazing glow-worms flicker here and there;
And the blueish wreath of the distant Apennines
Above whose summit dreams the yellow moon.

"My master!" Donatello pleads, "My dearest friend!"
The old man's eyes, filled with the sparkling rays
His soul absorbed from the glimmering skies,
Are fixed upon the pupil's pallid cheeks.
"I waited for you, Donatello, come!"
The pupil grasps the outstretched bony hand
The master offers him in welcoming,
And in a voice with passion tremulous
Pours out in words the burden of his soul:
"Father and friend and teacher most sublime,
You, who have guided my uncertain steps
Across the stony, steep and winding road
That leads men to the dizzy heights of fame,
Upon your soul's salvation, answer me!

307

Ty viděl's dílo moje, sochu mou?
Já vložil vše, co cítí duše má,
své bolesti, svůj vzlet, své hvězdné sny,
a sílu veškerou a nadšení,
a souhrn myšlenek, *vše,* v dílo to! . . .
Můj duch měl velkou, smělou vidinu:
chtěl dosáhnout, co nelze dosáhnout
snad nikdy smrtelnému člověku —
chtěl dílo *dokonalé* vytvořit!

To hrdé slovo jest snad rouháním?
Snad řekneš mi, že dílo takové
jen z bezdna záhadného rodí se,
z něhož jak lotus vykvet' tento svět,
že bez vady jen to, co tvoří Bůh,
že svatou jest to jeho výsadou.
Proč ale vložil pak do ňader mých
tu snahu nesmírnou po nejvyšším?
Ne, nevznítil tu jiskru génia,
by pouze hluše ve mně doutnala
a věčnou byla mukou, ne, on chtěl,
by vyšlehla jak slunce v plný žár! . . .
Nuž vím, že vykonala ruka má
to největší, co vykonat mi lze;
kam ted' mne nedones' můj ducha let,
tam nedolétnu nikdy, nikdy víc! . . .
Můj mistře, hle, já skláním hlavu svou,
necht' pronesou tvá ústa volný soud!
Jest dílem dokonalým výtvor můj?
A není-li, co chybí soše mé?"

Když Donatello takto domluvil,
vtisk' na ústa mu mistr polibek,
pak vnořil zrak svůj ve zrak jinocha
a odpověděl s jemným úsměvem:

„Můj Donatello, ty's to řek', ne já,
Bůh sám jen tvoří díla bez vady
a soše tvojí jedna chybí věc —
však neřeknu ti která, hádej sám.
Až uhodneš, pak opět ke mně přijd'."

You saw my work, the statue hewn of stone.
I placed therein all that my soul could feel;
My pains, my daring flight, my starry dreams,
And all the strength and fervor of my youth;
My very thoughts, my all, I placed therein.
My soul possessed a daring, mighty dream.
It would attain what cannot be attained
By any mortal man upon this earth . . .
I would create a perfect work of art.

"These haughty words, perhaps, are blasphemy?
Perhaps you'll say to me, 'Such perfect work
Can only rise from the deep unknown
From whence the world bloomed as a lotus bud;
That faultless is the work of God alone
To whom it is a sacred privilege.'
Then why did he implant within my soul
This boundless yearning, striving for the heights?
He did not light the spark of genius
That it should smoulder in me aimlessly,
As an eternal torment? No. He chose
That it should blossom like the glowing sun!
I know my hands have fashioned all they could,
The highest point to which I can aspire;
And heights to which my spirit has not soared,
I shall not reach nor ever more attain!
My master, see, I humbly bow my head.
Now let your lips their judgement freely pass.
Tell me if perfect is the work I have done.
If not, what is it that my statue lacks?"

When Donatello finished thus his plea,
The master placed a kiss upon his lips;
He deeply gazed into the youth's sad eyes
And with a gentle smile thus answered him.
"My Donatello, you, not I, have said
That God alone creates without a fault.
There is but one thing that your marble lacks . . .
I will not tell you what. That you must solve,
When you have found the answer, come again to me!"

309

To slovo těžce učně ranilo,
však mlčky beze vzdechu odešel
a mistr netušil, že mráz a tma
do duše Donatella vnikaly.
Od oné doby jímá choroba
a tajný smutek mysl umělce;
po úsměvu již není stopy víc
ni kolem rtů, ni v zracích zapadlých.
Po celé dny před sochou rozjímá
a dumá, hloubá v trapném neklidu
a hledá vady, najde tolik jich,
až posléz se mu socha celá zdá
být s temena do paty omylem!
Tu sřítila se lepá budova,
již Donatello stavěl z pyšných snů,
a pochovala v rumu trosek svých,
co nesmrtného bylo v umělci,
a nezbylo z té velké bytosti
než pouze to, co prachu náleží,
a Donatello kráčel smrti vstříc . . .
Juž nemá síly překročiti práh,
juž sedí mezi dveřmi na slunci
jak vetchý kmet, přec ještě upíná
svůj mroucí zrak na velké dílo své,
a ti, již kolem nešťastného jdou,
ti kropí ruku jeho slzami,
a dívky kladou růže v jeho klín,
jak zemřelým se hází do hrobky . . .

A přišel den, kdy klesl na lůžko,
by z něho nikdy více nepovstal;
tu vzkáže Donatello mistrovi,
by k němu přišel s ním se rozloučit.
A mistr vejde v tichou komnatu,
kam zlatě proudí teplý slunce svit,
kam z zahrad vniká sladký kosů zpěv,
by potěšily ještě naposled
to mroucí srdce trpce zklamané.

The words cut deeply through the pupil's heart,
But silently, without a sigh he left,
Nor did the master know what biting frost
Crept slowly into Donatello's soul.
From that night on, illness and secret grief
Now settled on the artist's burdened mind;
No trace remains of his once cheerful smile
Around his lips, nor in the sunken eyes.
Day after day he prods and meditates
Before the statue, musing restlessly,
Seeking its faults and finding more and more,
Until, at length, the statue seems to him
One huge mistake throughout its stony mass
To the dust of his hopes crumbles the edifice
Fashioned by Donatello from his dreams,
Burying in the ruin's smouldering dust
All that was once immortal in the man.
And of his being nothing more remains
But that which slowly turns to dust again,
And Donatello sadly faces death . . .
He even lacks the strength to leave his rooms,
And sits all day within the sunlit door,
An infirm, aged man, whose dying eyes
Are fastened far beyond, upon his towering work,
And those who pass his feeble staring form
Bathe with their tears his blue-veined, wasted hands;
And maidens shower roses in his lap,
Like flowers thrown within a gaping grave . . .

At last there came the day he took to bed
From which he never more would rise again;
And Donatello for his master sends
To come to him, to bid a last farewell.
The master comes within the silent room,
Where stream, like gold, the warm rays of the sun
And where the black-birds' sparkling song is heard
As if to cheer once more, with song and light
The sadly disillusioned, dying heart.

311

Bol nesmírný tu mistra zachvátí:
„Co trápilo tě, duše andělská,
co tvého žití liliový květ
tak zlomilo, že já, já vetchý kmet
nad tvojí rakví šedé vlasy rvu?"

A Donatello takto odpoví:
„Než zemru, mistře, rychle odpověz!
Ty řekl's mi, že chybí soše mé
jen jedna věc, ó, která jest to věc?"

A mistr na to: „Mluva chybí jí!" . . .

Tu vzkřikne Donatello jásavě
a oko jeho vzplane blaženstvím.
„Pak zemru štasten!" šeptá mistrovi
a usíná bez bolu v věčný sen,
jak pták usíná zpěvem znavený,
když za horami slunce zapadne. —

The master speaks, his voice is filled with grief;
"What pain tormented you, angelic soul?
What broke the lily blossom of your life?
What grieved you so that I, an aged man,
Above your death-bed tear my snow-white hair?"

And Donatello feebly answers him;
Before I die, my master, quickly speak!
You said my statue lacks one thing alone.
What is this need? What is the fault you saw?"

The master speaks: "All that it lacks is speech."

Then Donatello cries with reborn joy,
His eyes once more are lit with happiness.
He whispers faintly: "Happily I die."
At peace he slips away to eternal dreams
As a bird, worn out by singing, falls asleep
When the sun has set beyond the mountain tops.

313

*B*y 1880 the taste of the literary public seems to have turned against the Parnassian school, of which Vrchlický was still the most eminent living representative. They were charged with verbalism, hollow rhetoric and aestheticism; an adoration of art for its own sake; and a blindness towards real contemporary issues. It was natural that a generation which, by artistic discipline has perfected a form of literature should be disowned by successors who react from the cult of discipline to that of freedom, and from the search for formal perfection to a desire for a cruder realism: the trend in art was parallelled by a revulsion of feeling against the romantic nationalism which had become fashionable. The greatest single figure of the Realist movement among the Czechs was not a poet but a philosopher, teacher, prose writer, critic, and finally a states-man—T. G. Masaryk: a reaction against artistry and formalism might well be expected to include a reaction against poetry as such; but in the Czech case this did not happen. Czech Realism had a strong response in poetry; its best-known representatives remain Petr Bezruč and JOSEF SVATOPLUK MACHAR (1864-1942). Machar's poetic corpus is rather large and of uneven quality. In style his work seeks contact with the vernacular and does not avoid dissonance or ugliness. Disillusion, scepticism, and sarcasm are features of his approach; and in a desire to mirror contemporary reality he brings to poetry the themes of human deprivation and brutality. It is a type of political poetry, in which the poet sees himself not as the prophet of his people, but in the less elevated role of society's critic. Machar wrote personal lyrics, usually of a gloomy and pessimistic kind, in which death was a common motif. Later he attempted an ambitious epic on the theme of man's history, from the earliest times until today. It is a mark of Machar's pessimism, and of his attitude to institutionalised religion, that he placed the highlight of human achievement in classical culture, and saw in Christianity an influence for decay. Machar is one of the few Czech poets to write with success on the theme of man's corruption by ideology,—national, political, and religious. He is, above all, an individualist.

315

V SENTIMENTÁLNÍM MLÁDÍ

Josef
Svatopluk
Machar
(1864-1942)

V sentimentálním mládí milovali
jsme podzimky a žlutých listů pád,
a šedé mlhy, které napadaly
pustnoucích do zahrad.

A ted' má člověk rád
to velké slunce, jež se v obzor valí
v glorii blesků, rád dnů žhavých řad,
zem sžíhanou, jež pod nohama pálí.

Když podzimek ted' slzný krajem táhne,
mha špinavá kdy všude rozložena,
náladu očistce kde nese každý z dnů, —

po zlatém víně ruka ráda sáhne:
v něm je ta záře slunce uzavřena,
žár července a blaho letních snů!

AUTUMN SONNET

We in our sentimental salad-days
Loved autumn, and the leafage drooping sere,
And the descent of misty greys
On gardens growing drear.

But now these things to man are dear:
The mighty sun, that on the sky-line sways
In glory; and the days in warm career,
The glow of earth beneath his feet ablaze.

When tearful autumn roves across the land,
And everywhere a parlous mist is poured,
And every day a purgatory seems —

We gladly clutch the wine-cup in our hand;
For there the ardour of the sun is stored,
Heat of July and bliss of summer dreams.

Translated
by Paul
Selver

DUMA

Josef
Svatopluk
Machar

Jen několik let — — kosti vykopají
a pohodí je někde v kostnici,
kdy písní mojich zvuky téż se stají,
jak v háji zpěv, když zmizí slavíci.

Zda potom někdo vezme prázdnou lebku
jak Hamlet ve svou chvějící se dlaň
a zahledí se mých dum na kolebku,
jež přírodě svou zaplatila daň?

Zda vyčte myšlenek tam různých sledy,
muk lásky pozná a všech strastí byt,
zda poví mu ten čelisti kruh bledý,
że i to čelo vavřín chtělo mít?

Zda otáže se, kde ten duch, jenž plaše
chtěl perutí až k hvězdám povzletnout?
Eh! přeříká snad kousek otčenáše
a sinou lebku hodí v tmavý kout!

BROODING

A few more years, — and they will drag my bones,
And let them in a charnel-house be shed,
After my melodies have hushed their tones,
Mute as a grove, whence nightingales have fled.

Will someone then the empty skull upraise
Upon his trembling hand, with Hamlet's view
Amid the cradle of my dreams to gaze,
That has to nature paid its final due?

Will he mark out each divers track of thought,
The irk of love, and all the anguish there?
And will the pallid jawbone tell him aught
Of laurels that this brow was fain to wear?

And will he wonder where the soul may lag
That once urged on its wings to starward flight?
Pooh! He will mumble forth some pious tag,
And cast the livid skull away from sight!

Translated
by Paul
Selver

POSEL

Josef
Svatopluk
Machar

Ó Spart'ané, já spěchám od Thermopyl.
Mě Leonidas vyslal umíraje . . .

. . . A padli všichni? . . .
                              . . . Po zákonech vlasti.
A těla barbarská se kol nich kupí
jak hory a s těch sláva Lakoniky
větrnou nohou po Helladě běží . . .
. . . A můj syn Agil? . . .
                              . . . Jako včely v úl svůj
tak spěla kopí perská v prsa jeho . . .
. . . Já smrtelného zrodila jsem syna.
Ó bozi věční, ted' jsem matkou šťastnou! . . .

. . . Tak. Pravdu díš. Však neblahý já posel,
jenž slepým losem určen k službě trudné
jsem místo svoje opustiti musil,
kam poději se? Budu potácet se
ve světle denním, živá kořist Hádu,
a zhrda všech jen údělem mým bude.
A když pak zemru, nikým neželen,
stín osamělý, Hádem bloudit budu,
neb druzí z boje víc mne nepoznají,
a k nim se hlásit sám—stud zabrání mi. . . .

320

THE MESSENGER

"Spartans, from Thermopylae I run;
Leonidas that sent me, as he died . . ."
"Then all have fallen? . . ."
                              "As their homeland's writ
Had bidden them. Around, barbaric dead
Lie heaped like mountains. Thence, on airy foot,
Laconian glory speeds through Hellas' land."
"My son Agil . . . ?"
                              "Like bees that seek their hive,
So flew a Persian spear within his breast . . ."
". . . My son . . . he was a mortal. O ye gods
Eternal, now I feel a mother's joy."

"Why, so. Well spoken. Yet no blessing rests
On me the courier, whom a sightless chance
Has sentenced to this melancholy task,
Compelled to leave my post. And whither now?
To wander in the light of day, the spoil
Of Hades, living on; and, for my lot,
Contempt from all. And, when I die, unmourned,
A lonely shade through Hades' halls to stray;
My comrades from the fight shall know me not,
And shame will let me call to them no more."

Translated
by Alfred
French

*T*he fame of *PETR BEZRUČ (1867-1958) rests, in effect, on one book, Silesian Songs, containing 31 poems and first published in 1903. The main themes of his verse—protest against social injustice and foreign oppression—might be expected severely to date his work and limit its appeal. And yet in spite of his limited output and of its local and temporal interest, Bezruč has achieved a lasting popularity and a prominent place in Czech literature. The paradox is typical of the writer, who concealed a refined poetic technique under a raw exterior; combined dignity and pathos with an unsentimental crudity of expression; and could turn a hymn of hate into a true lyric poem.*

In later life Bezruč wrote personal lyrics, but they lack the power of his earlier, more socially-orientated work. At his best he essays the hard role of the poet as the voice, and the prophet, of his people. Consequently he attempts to efface himself from his art, at the same time shunning all prettiness and overt charm. He compared his poetry to the cactus flower, which issues from harsh spikes of the plant, and blossoms in the darkness where few can see it. By its force and originality his poetry was a startling contribution to the Czech literary scene around the turn of the century. It is likely to live; because it expresses in direct form and limited content ideas which the reader recognises as universal, and feelings which correspond to his own.

JÁ, PETR BEZRUČ

Petr Bezruč
(1864-1958)

Já, Petr Bezruč, od Těšína Bezruč,
toulavý šumař a bláznivý gajdoš,
šílený rebel a napilý zpěvák,
zlověstný sýček na těšínské věži,
hraju a zpívám, co kladiva duní
z Vítkovic, z Frydlantu, pod Lipinami.
Kolem jdou bohatci cizí mi víry,
(Bezruči Petře, jak je máš rád!)
mužové slavných a vznešených názvů,
skvělí jak bozi a hrdí jak hvězdy,
(Bezruči Petře, kdo ubil tvou ves?),
kolem jdou v hedvábí, v atlase dámy,
kolem jdou mužové vážní i mocní,
mocní na Dunaji, ve Zlatém městě,
kolem jdou básníci z vltavských břehu,
co milují ženy, jak kázala Paříž,
pod smyčcem zoufalá chvěje se struna,
těžký dech sedmdesáti tisíců,
kamenům zpívám a balvanům hraju,
hraju a zpívám—tož dáte mi krejcar?

324

Handwritten notes:

sýček : little owl
mocnost: power
atlase : sotin
NÁZEV title / name
zoufalí : in despair
hedvábí silk, rayon

I, PETR BEZRUČ

I, Petr Bezruč, Bezruč of Těšin—
wandering fiddler and crazy bagpiper,
mad rebel and drunken singer,
owl of ill-omen on the towers of Těšin—
I play and sing while the hammers thunder
in Vítkovice, Frýdlant and under Lipina.
Around me go the rich, no kin of mine,
(Petr Bezruč, how you love them!)
men who are famous, of lordly line,
proud as the stars, splendid as gods,
(Petr Bezruč, who wiped out your village?)
before me go ladies in velvet and silk,
around me the men of power and fame
from the golden city beside the Danube,
and the long-haired poets from the Vltava's banks,
lovers of fair women as Paris instructed.
The one string of my fiddle quivers despairing
with the heavy sigh of the seventy thousand,
I sing to the stones, I play to the rocks,
I play and I sing—will you toss me a penny?

Translated
by Ian
Milner

325

OSTRAVA

Petr
Bezruč

Sto roků v šachtě žil, mlčel jsem,
sto roků kopal jsem uhlí,
za sto let v rameni bezmasém
svaly mi v železo ztuhly.

Uhelný prach sed mi do očí,
rubíny ze rtů mi uhly,
se vlasů, s vousů a s obočí
visí mi rampouchy uhlí.

Chléb s uhlím beru si do práce,
z roboty jdu na robotu,
při Dunaji strmí paláce
z krve mé a z mého potu.

Sto roků v kopalně mlčel jsem,
kdo mi těch sto roků vrátí?
Když jsem jim pohrozil kladivem,
kdekdo se začal mi smáti.

Abych měl rozum, šel v kopalnu zas,
pro pány dřel se jak prve—
napřáh jsem kladivo—teklo v ráz
na Polské Ostravě krve!

Všichni vy na Slezské, všichni vy, dím,
nech je vám Petr neb Pavel,
mějž prs kryt krunýřem ocelovým,
tisícům k útoku zavel;

všichni vy na Slezské, všichni vy, dím,
hlubokých páni vy dolů;
přijde den, z dolů jde plamen a dým,
přijde den, súčtujem spolu!

OSTRAVA

A hundred years mute I lived in the pit,
a hundred years I dug the coal,
a hundred years on my lean arms were knit
muscles of iron mould.

Translated
by Ian
Milner

My eyes the coal-dust has clogged and seared,
the red has gone from my lips,
and from my eyebrows, hair and beard
hang the black icicle tips.

Coal-bitter is the bread I bring to eat,
day after day I drudge,
from my blood and from my sweat
palaces spring by the Danube's edge.

A hundred years in the pit I held my tongue,
who will return them to me?
When hammer on high I strode among
them they answered with mockery:

Come to your senses, get back to the pit,
sweat as we masters summon—
down swung my hammer—the swift blood from it
through the streets of Ostrava ran!

All you in Silesia, I speak to you all,
miner and every manjack,
put on your shield and buckler of steel,
call thousands to the attack;

All you in Silesia, all you I name,
who own the mines as your due:
the day is coming, in smoke and in flame,
the day we shall reckon with you!

SLEZSKÉ LESY

Petr
Bezruč

Jste tak jak já, slezské lesy, mé lesy!
Smutek se na kmen a koruny věsí,
hledíte teskno a hledíte přísně,
jak moje myšlenky, jak moje písně.
Padá z vás jehličí v noci a v mlze,
porobeného to národa slze.

Padáte sekerou na rozkaz z Vídně,
hynete pomalu, hynete klidně!
Mlčíte, hynete, smrkové moře,
bez konce, bez konce slezké vy hoře!

SILESIAN FORESTS

You are like me, my Silesian forests!
Sorrow clings to your trunks and crests,
sad your look is, sombre your gaze,
just as my thoughts, just as my lays.
Your needles fall through the night to the ground,
tears of a nation crushed and bound.

The axe fells you at Vienna's decree,
and you die slowly, you die calmly!
In silence you vanish, ocean of pine,
unending, unending, your grief and mine!

Translated
by Ian
Milner

329

KDO NA MOJE MÍSTO?

Petr
Bezruč

Tak málo mám krve a ještě mi teče
z úst.
Až bude růst
nade mnou tráva, až budu hnít,
kdo na moje místo,
kdo zdvihne můj štít?

V dým zahalen vítkovských pecí jsem stál,
noc zřela mi z očí, plam z nozdry mi vál,
nech zářilo slunce, nech večer se šeřil,
já semknutou brvou jsem vrahy ty měřil:
ty bohaté židy, ty grófy* ze šlachty,
já škaredý kovkop, jak vyskočil z šachty.
Nech diadem jednomu na skráni svítil,
každý z nich upjatý pohled můj cítil,
mou zaťatou pěst, můj vzdor,
hněv kovkopa z Bezkyd a z hor. —

Tak málo mám krve a ještě mi teče
z úst.
Až bude růst
nade mnou tráva, až budu hnít,
kdo místo mne na stráž,
kdo zdvihne můj štít?

330

WHO COMES IN MY PLACE?

Translated
by Alfred
French

I have so little blood,
And yet, down from my mouth
How it flows!
When there grows spreading grass on my grave,
When I rot in the field,
Who comes then in my place?
Who will lift up my shield?

I stood shrouded in smoke from the furnaces' glow,
With the night in my eyes, with the flame in my breath,
In the light of the sun, in the evening gloom;
And I scowled as I measured the killers within;
The Jews with their wealth and the lords with their rank,
I repulsive—a miner still foul from the pit.
Though a head gave the flash of a diadem bright,
Yet they sensed my defiance, the first that I clenched.
Then each one, at my gaze, with uneasiness fills,
At the hate of a miner from Beskydan hills.

I have so little blood,
And yet down from my mouth
How it flows!
When there grows spreading grass on my grave,
When I rot in the field,
Who will stand at my post?
Who will lift up my shield?

331

abcdefghijklmno
!'pqrstuvwxyz?

1 2 3 4 5
6 7 8 9 0

The last decade of the XIXth century saw the literary debut of a group of writers who, because of common traits and outlook, have come to be regarded as a separate literary generation. It was they who emphasised their separateness, rejecting with scorn and contumely the most cherished values of their elders. 'We have looked with scepticism upon our fathers. A sorry sight!' Such were the words of the Manifesto of Czech Modernism published in 1895. Pious faith in liberal humanism; an optimistic trust in national virtue; lofty poetic diction, and pretentious rhetoric in art—such were the symptoms of the living style which the angry young writers sought to sweep into oblivion. The common platform for their own work was the journal The Modern Revue; and from it they set out to revolutionise art, and with art, life.

A member of the group which signed the manifesto was ANTONIN SOVA (1864-1928). In style he reacted against the elevated diction of the Parnassians by bringing the language of poetry closer to that of contemporary prose. In spirit he spoke for the solitary individualist, alienated by his rejection of current social values: his is the voice of the 'lost generation.' Sova's poetry includes intimate lyrics clouded with melancholy and self-questioning; love poems; impressionist cameos of natural landscapes, and mental anguish. In his later work he essayed grander themes of a utopian future expressed through mystical visions, so that his work is often coupled with that of his contemporary Otokar Březina. But Sova's greatest success was with the short lyric, striking in its mastery of sound effects, and in its brevity; and presenting a daunting challenge to any would-be translator.

333

PÍSEŇ

Antonín
Sova
(1864-1928)

Já housle vzal jsem v ruku
po letech doma zas!
Tak neuměle, tiše
zvuk nesmělý se třás!
Zvuk nesmělý se třás—
já hrát již zapomněl,
ó marno! vzpomínám si,
já hrát již zapomněl!

A v žádosti a touze
po měkkých houslích svých,
jež plakaly tak dlouze
za nocí měsíčních—
za nocí měsíčních!—
já silněj v struny vjel,
ó marno, struna praskla,
já hrát již zapomněl!

I ta, jež ráda měla
můj hovor dumavý,
se ani nezachvěla,
zrak nevzplál pátravý!
Zrak nevzplál pátravý
po letech, jaký žel!
Já zestár jsem a dávno
jsem líbat zapomněl!

334

TOUHA Lmým-
HOVOR - TALK   žel -   ŽAL - sad nostalga

A SONG

I took the fiddle in my hand:
for years had passed, and I was home.
Then faint and artless came the sound—
a timid, quavering tone!
A timid, quavering tone—
I had forgotten how to play.
So hopeless! I remembered then,
I had forgotten how to play.

And longing, oh so fervently
for the mellow, stringed delights
of that drawn-out weeping melody
from the distant, moonlit nights—
from the distant moonlit nights!—
I tried to make the strings obey.
So hopeless! For the string had snapped.
I had forgotten how to play.

And the one who loved my musings once,
and touched my words with grace,
she gave no sign, made no response;
no radiance crossed her face.
No radiance crossed her face:
time brings its nemesis;
for years had passed and I was old.
I had forgotten how to kiss.

Translated
by Alfred
French

335

JEŠTĚ JEDNOU SE VRÁTÍME . . .

Antonín
Sova Ještě jednou se vrátíme zamyšleni, kde prudce
květ voněl, že svedl nás z cesty, když šeřivým stříbrem tekl
nad potoky večer, a ještě jednou se vrátíme,
kde píseň jsme slyšeli z oken, jež hleděla k zahradám zmlklým.

A ještě si vynajdem jednu stezku a jeden háj v horách
tak celý podzimem jasný, v tolika hýřících barvách,
po roztříštěných akordech echa budeme pátrat,
po tichém a pružném kroku, zda tajemné zanechal stopy.

Duše, do níž se zařízly vzpomínky, vyleje v trávu
tolik lyriky kanoucí v pryskyřičných krůpějích,
své větve vysoké, tmavé vykoupá v podzimním slunci,
svůj štíhlý kmen protáhne šerem v mijící mraky;–
to všecko v jediné chvíli, na stezce sešeřené
a v hodinu západu, která tak sevře nebohé srdce.

ONCE MORE IN THOUGHT WE'LL RETURN

Once more in thought we'll return, where the heavy fragrance
      of flowers
Lured us away from the road, when evening in lilac and silver
Flowed over meadow and stream, once more the song shall
      enchant us
That fell from the open window, on the garden charmed into
      silence.
Yet once again we'll discover one pathway, one wood in the
      mountains,
All incandescent with autumn, in so many riotous colours.
After the ruined chords we shall seek out the lingering echoes,
After the soft, light step, we shall look for the secret
      footprints.

The soul, impaled on its memories, pours out in the grass of
      the meadow
So many lyrical fancies, dropping in resinous tears,
Its branches, lofty and sombre, are bathed in the autumn
      sunlight,
Its slender trunk threads a twilight, a gloom of passing cloud-
      shadows;
All in one moment of time, here on the darkening pathway,
When the sunset hour overwhelms the heart with its burden
      of sorrow.

Translated
by E.
Pargeter

*Pozdravujeme jaro! Máme netrpělivost duší!
Tresení křídel sesílených! Odvahu vraku ja svěléko!
Nekonečnosti čekají na nás, jitra, slavnější jara,
věčnosti hřmící písně, vysvobození!*

Otokar Březina.

*T*he name OTOKAR BŘEZINA *(1868-1929) is generally coupled with that of Antonín Sova as the two most eminent representatives of Czech symbolism in poetry. The term 'symbolism' is
not altogether a happy one, since it stresses only one aspect of
their work—the allusive use of words to conjure up a world of
diverse associations. The Czech symbolists were much influenced
by the techniques of musical composition; and they explored the
possibilities of sounds and objects in evoking unexpressed meaning.
As the Parnassians had temporarily exhausted the possibilities of
conventional poetic form, so the symbolists, aided by the example
of the modern French poets, opened the way for fresh experimen-
tation. Shunning the ugliness of the man-made world Březina writes
of the mystery and silence of the cosmos: the personality of the
artist is submerged in the common experience of all sentient things;
and the passing moment is set in the context of eternity. Although
Březina is not often considered as a personal poet, his lyric poetry
is essentially the product of his private, dream world; and it is often
expressed via so many layers of meaning as frequently to baffle or
lose the reader. Březina's verse is heavily influenced by his reading
of philosophy, both ancient and modern: at times he seems to view
the artist as a mediator between man and the vast, but unperceived,
areas of reality which lie below the level of surface phenomena. In
Březina the poet briefly resumed an ancient role as the seer, initiat-
ed by his inner, mystical experience, and returning, like Orpheus
from the dead, to tell of metaphysical horizons unvisited by man.
In Western Europe the swing of the pendulum from realist to impressionist literature came only after the realists had exhausted the
novelty of their approach. But the end of the century in Bohemia
saw a simultaneous growth of both realism, and a symbolism which,
in the case of Březina, was akin to metaphysical romanticism.*

339

ZEM?

Otokar
Březina
(1868-1929)

Svět rozkládá se za světem,
   za hvězdou hvězda, když půlnoc se tmí,
   a mezi nimi je jeden, krouží kolem bílého slunce,
   a let jeho hudbou tajemné radosti hřmí,
   a duše těch, kteří nejvíce trpěli,
   do něho vejíti smí.

Sta bratří řeklo: Známe tajemství jeho,
   mrtví v něm vstávají ze sna, živí v něm zmírají snem;
   milenci řekli: Přílišnou září oslepli zraky
   a čas jako vůně neznámých květů každého usmrtí v něm;
   a ti, kteří dovedli viděti tisíciletí,
   s úsměvem ptají se: Zem?

IS THIS EARTH?

World upon world looms up,
Star upon star in midnight's dark reign,
And one in their midst abides, round a dazzling orb it circles,
And the sound of its flight is a joyous and baffling refrain,
And the souls of them who have suffered the most
May enter within its domain.

Brethren by hundreds have said: We have fathomed its secret,
There do the dead from slumber arise, in slumber the quick
       pass away;
Lovers have said: Its surfeit of lustre will blind us
And time, like fragrance of blossoms unknown, all its
       dwellers will slay:
And those whose vision has power to range through the ages,
Is this earth? they smilingly say.

Translated
by Paul
Selver

ZPÍVALY HOŘÍCÍ HVĚZDY

Otokar
Březina

Každou vteřinou, vždy na svém místě
v mystickém tanci světů
kroužíme kosmem.
V zářící sféry duchů sáláme svůdné
krásou.
Kolem hlav našich,
aureolami
zlaté vlasy se jiskří,
napínané jak zvonící lasa
vichřicí letu.

Do tváří našich, jež v extási hoří,
chladivě věky nám vanou
a schvácené štěstím letu svého,
zářením bolestné rozkoše vysílené,
s výkřikem, jenž letí nekonečnem,
harmonický a jásající,
klesáme, mystické tanečnice,
a v krvi své, jako pohřbené v růžích,
umíráme.

Vstupují sestry na naše místo,
běloskvoucí,
a v písni, jež soumraky věčna se valí,
vlnami stále vzrůstajícími,
v nové a nové prostory postupuje
v mlhovin prachu pozdviženém,
zářící předvoj mystéria.

THUS SANG THE BURNING STARS

Each instant, ever within our places
Amid mystical dancing of worlds
We circle through the cosmos.
Into spirits' radiant spheres we blaze alluring
With beauty.
Around our heads
In aureoles
Sparkle golden tresses,
Stretched like resonant lassos
By flight's whirlwind.

Into our faces, burning with ecstasy,
Breathes ages' chillness
And clutched by our flight's rapture,
Overpowered by dazzle of grievous bliss,
With outcry, that scours the unbounded,
Harmonious, exulting,
We sink, mystical dancers,
And in our blood, as if buried in roses,
We perish.

Sisters arise in our places,
White-shimmering,
And in song, that soars through eternity's twilights,
With ever increasing billows,
Anew and anew into spaces
Amid upraised dust of nebulas,
The mystery's gleaming advance-guard.

Translated
by Paul
Selver

JARNÍ NOC

Otokar
Březina

Noc tiše zpívala, šum prvních zelení a jarních vod
byl její melancholické písně doprovod;
ve výši hvězdy, světelné kalichy nesmírné,
dýchaly těžkou vůni nadzemských vegetací;
a ruce bratří mých, jak při smrti na prsou zkřížené,
ležely tiché a zklamané a jako kámen ztížené
zlomeny prací.

Však jejich ruce duchové k hvězdám se rozepjaly,
miliony duší na zemi a ve všech světech objaly
a dlouhý oddech radostných procitnutí,
sváteční vření věčného města,
duchových křidel šumění, hra větrů v mystickém osení,
orchestrů neviditelných zapění,
zdvihlo se v taktu jejich tajuplného gesta.

344

SPRING NIGHT

The night sang quietly; and Spring's first shoots,
her murmuring streams, accompanied the solemn melody;
the stars above, like radiant goblets vast,
breathed in from growth unearthly heavy scent;
my brethren's arms lay crossed upon their breast
subdued, as if in death, weighed down, at rest,
by heavy labour spent.

Yet they to stars their ghostly arms were holding,
a million souls in the universe enfolding,
and the long relief of waking joy,
the eternal city's festive symphony,
through ghostly sowing the breeze, unearthly wings,
from unseen orchestras the strings,
to their mystic gesture moved in harmony.

Translated
by Alfred
French

345

Karel Hlaváček's illustration of his own volume of poetry,
Pozdě k ránu (1896)

*I*n their differing ways the realists and the symbolists both expressed the artists' aversion to the materialistic values of nineteenth century society. But this attitude of contempt and hatred was carried further by a group of Czech poets who modelled their style on the French self-styled Decadents.

To the Decadents art was the last refuge before the flood, a method of escape from the hideousness of contemporary life, and a platform from which to abuse a society which ignored or derided them. They aimed at the oblivious ears of the bourgeois their exaltation of free love and Satanism: seeing no chance to live as they wished, they glorified death, and made decay and ruin their favourite subject—the beauty of flowers which soon must wither; of the young because they soon must age and die; of the past because it is a monument to transience, decay, and the futility of man's endeavours. The platform of the Decadent movement was The Modern Revue, which set itself in the vanguard of aesthetic, life. The two most talented poets of the movement were JIŘÍ KARÁSEK (1871-1951) and KAREL HLAVÁČEK (1874-1898). Karásek, once dubbed a king of poseurs, was a prolific writer, and the titles of some of his books have a bizarre—almost comic—ring to modern ears: Bricked-up Windows; Sodom; Aristocratic Book; and Sexus necans (subsequently republished in the collection Talks with Death).

The decadents drew into their ranks writers who shared with them a brief honeymoon of luxurious nihilism, then went their own way; they include the poet S. K. Neumann, subsequently anarchist, vitalist, and communist in his affiliations, and Viktor Dyk, who was to become the fiery spokesman of Czech nationalism. They called themselves the lost generation; and although they have been rightly accused of putting illusion before reality, they did, in their own eccentric way, stand up for the importance and self-justification of art. Subsequent generations which have been sickened by the eagerness of writers to serve with their talents political or social pressure groups, have recognised with gratitude the genuine voice of poetry in these theatrical bohemians. All their poses and gestures were exaggerated—scepticism, irony, nihilism, contempt for others, rejection of society. Their cultivated attitudes were crammed together in a small space to form a literary genre which a critic subsequently termed the "illusionist baroque."

PŘÍŠERNÁ LOĎ

Jiří Karásek
ze Lvovic
(1871-1951)

V neznámých mořích neznámých zemí
Na mrtvých vodách hluboký klid.
V zsinalém nebi měsíční štít
Bez lesku, bez barvy, smutný a němý.

Veliký koráb, s plachtami všemi
Černými stářím, přestal se chvít
Na mrtvých vodách. Začíná hnít.
Dlouho tu, dlouho již, smutný a němý ...

V kajutách slyšet zdušený škyt.
Nejasné stíny palubou chodí.
Děsno a příšerno po celé lodi.

Náhrobní lampa, měsíční štít,
Vápenně v tváře zelené plaje
Lodníkům zlákaným v Neznáma kraje.

THE SPECTRAL SHIP

In oceans unfathomed, of regions unknown.
Upon the dead waters deep silences weigh.
In a livid heaven the moonlight's array
Is lack-lustre, hueless, eerie and lone.

A mighty vessel, with sails that are grown
Darksome with age, has long ceased to sway
Upon the dead waters. Now dawns its decay.
Long, long has it been here, silent and lone.

In the cabin a stifled gasp of dismay.
Over the deck dim shadows tread.
The ship is utterly spectral and dread.

A funereal lantern, the moonlight's array
Chalkily shines on the greenish faces
Of mariners lured to Uncharted Places.

Translated
by Paul
Selver

UPÍR

Karel Hlaváček (1874-1898)

Bylo to v jakési temné krajině
se zlatou skvrnou luny kdes nahoře za mraky,
v krajině neznámé, bázlivé, rozplizlé, bez stínu, bez světla,
kterou jsem nikdy doposud nešel,
když jsem ho zhléd. . .

Mihl se nízko a tiše nade mnou,
v bledých barvách jemné a staré litografie.
Znavený jeho obličej, sličný a bledý,
na čele se svítilnou očí zelených pod srostlým obočím
bázlivé černé oči mé provždy atropinoval. . .
Nesl se tiše v páru svých upířích křídel,
kovově černých a sametných, napnutých v obrovském rámu,
jež stínily celou oblohu
a pod jejichž rozmachy prýskaly hvězdy
bez vzruchu, jak žhavý roj divokých, kovových včel
z osykového pralesa vichřicí vyplašených. . .
Poslední potomek mocných kdys rodů vévodských
neznámou letěl krajinou,
v návratu od svojich vášnivých, bezděčných milenek,
na úzkých sevřených retech
jich teplé budoucí mateřské mléko a ňader jich krev.
Bylo to v temné jakési krajině,
bázlivé, se zlatou skvrnou měsíce,
kudy jsem doposud nikdy se neplížil,
když jsem ho zhléd. . .
Jeho, posledního suveréna, z mocného kdys tak rodu,
před nímž se bázní chvěli měšťané, magnáti, králové,
a jejichž dcerky pak tiché a stonavé
toužily po něm tajně měsíce, dny. . .
Toužily po jeho návštěvě za tichých nocí měsíčných,
kdy čekaly, až zakryjí jeho peruti horká jich lože,
až jejich bílým masem proběhne jeho přítomnost
a až jeho lepkavý, drsný jazyk v bolestném pocitu na ňadrech
jim zatrhá sladce chorými víčky oči zanícených.

350

THE VAMPIRE

Translated
by Alfred
French

A weird pall lay on the land,
the moon rode high—a golden spot behind the clouds—
a strange and haunted landscape, foul, with neither shade
       nor light,
a place where I had never passed before,
when I caught sight of him. . .

In silence he came swooping overhead,
fine-etched against the sky, like an antique print,
his face exhausted, wan and beautiful,
below thick brows green eyes, whose torch
forever pierced my startled eyes with atropine. . .
He flew in silence, borne on vampire wings,
metallic black and velvet, spread in giant span
that shrouded all the sky:
beneath their arc a shower of stars,
In breathless hush, like swarm of wild metallic bees
a gale has lashed from age-old aspen glen. . .
Last scion of once powerful, princely clan
he flew above that unknown land
returning home from lovers unresisting, passionate,
whose pregnant breasts had flecked with milk, and blood,
his thin and tight-set lips.
A weird pall lay on the land,
a haunted place, with the moon a golden spot,
a place my stealthy feet had never trod,
when I caught sight of him. . .
Last ruler from once powerful clan,
before whose face had trembled burghers, magnates, kings,
whose daughters, mute and ailing, yearned
in secrecy for him as months and days went by. . .
They yearned through silent moonlit nights until he came
to cover with his wings their ardent couch,
to feel his presence pierce their pallid flesh,
his furry, clinging tongue upon their breasts,
to twitch the lids above their burning eyes
in agonising ecstasy.

351

Upír   Démone tajemných noci, nocí se zlatou skvrnou měsíce,
        nocí bázlivých, rozplizlých,
        nocí bez stínu, bez světla,
        se slabými záblesky lascívních primérních pudů na obzoru:
        Ty hrdý a bílý barbare, milenče všeho chorého, bledého,
        bezcitný a zase bázlivý, vznešený šílenče,
        jenž živíš se zbylou vitálnou silou panenských šť'áv,
        stižených dědičnou atrofií,
        symbole dekadence!
        Je brloh, kam přede dnem zalézáš,
        někde snad v černých krajinách *Vévodství* mého?
        Nevím to—
        ale zdá se mi za nocí tesklivých, podivných,
        že duše má dělí se od těla
        a najednou dostává upíří peruti,
        pod jejichž rozmachy prýskají bez vzruchu hvězdy,
        a krajinou bázlivou, rozplizlou, bez stínu, bez světla,
        se zlatou skvrnou měsíce nahoře kdesi za mraky,
        dává se tichounce v let.

        . . . A pozdě pak k ránu až, vrací se zmámená
        mystickou orgií—
        a procítá ve všedním parazitu,
        jenž bídně provleče zase den v profánním hluku ulice,
        jak bylo to v prokletém včerejšku
        a bude ve zhnuseném zítřku. . .

O demon of the secret nights, gold-spotted by the moon,
foul, haunted nights
with neither shade nor light,
faint-lit by distant flashes of primeval lust!
You pallid, proud barbarian; the paramour of lovers pale,
*   diseased,*
fear-haunted, callous, crazed, sublime,
that feed upon the ebbing vital power of maidenhood
whose deadly heritage is atrophy;
you symbol of all decadence!
The lair to which you shrink when night is done,
it may be that it lies within my Dukedom's gloomy lands?
I know not—yet it seems,
in the darkness of the lonely, eerie nights,
my spirit, parting from the flesh
takes sudden flight on vampire wings,
beneath whose arc floats, motionless, a shower of stars,
and through that haunted landscape foul, with neither shade
*   nor light,*
as the moon rides high, a golden spot behind the clouds,
he arises through the air in silent flight.

. . . And later, when the night is done, returns
by mystic orgies still bewitched—
to waken in the worldly parasite,
who languishes through one more day of earthly pandemonium,
like the ghoulish yesterday that was,
and the loathsome day that is to come. . .

353

O*TAKAR THEER (1880-1917) published his first book of verse at the age of 17, under the pseudonym of Otto Gulon. Entitled Woods Where There Is Dancing, the book contains some charming, sensuous lyrics, impregnated with languid irony of fin de siècle poetry. Theer's rather exclusive and aristocratic upbringing fitted him, even at this early stage, to adopt the aloof pose of the Decadents: later he travelled widely in Europe, spent a prolonged period in France, and won a reputation as a translator and critic. When, after a long break, he returned to creative writing, the young sensualist had matured into a highly intellectual writer: dedicating his work to Březina, he wrote lyrics of tragic anxiety and metaphysical vision. His compositions include Phaeton, an Aeschylean-type drama in verse, a story of heroic and doomed ambition. Theer is one of the writers who carried the artistic styles of nineteenth century literature into a new era, where the progress of events and changes of fashion already made them seem literary survivals, if not artistic curiosities.*

355

PODZIMNÍ NÁLADA

Otakar
Theer
(1880-1917)

Dal vítr ke rtům polnici
a zadul. Skučící
a štkavé, štěkavé a žalující—
jak smečky vydávání, pláč jak listí ve vichřici—
šly hlasy z jeho vykynulých lící.
Pak, v slunka úsměvu, se neslo utišení.
Vzplál v broskvích rudý strom a v révě zasvit' hrozen.
Checht zařehotal. . . Měchatý to Silén—
číš v pravici a zvadlé listí na lysině—
sem vpotácel se. . . Lehce po pěšině
se šoumá ženský krok, a tvrdě pazneht duní:
kozonoh s ženkou. S rohů se mu spouští
nit, babí léto. Ji věnec aster krášlí.
Zašli. . .
A ticho. . . Polibek jen slyšeti je v houšti
a na obzoru řev smečky se vzdalující.

AUTUMNAL

The wind with lifted bugle sent
Forth a gusty lament,
And sobs and snarls and cries of discontent,
Like an unleashed pack, like the wail of leaves that are
        tempest-rent,—
From the bulging cheeks of the wind these clamours went,
And then, amid the smiling of the sun, were lulled.
Redly blazed a peach-laden tree and a grape-vine shimmered.
A whinny of mirth arose. . . . It was paunchy Silenus,
Clutching a wine-cup, sere leaves on his hairless pate,
And reeling forward. . . . A woman's tripping gait
Stirs on the path, mingled with thud of a hoof:
A satyr and his quean. Gossamer wisps
Trail from his horns. Asters bedeck her head.
Their tread
Has faded. . . . Naught now is heard but dalliance in the
        spinney,
And on the sky-line waning howl of the pack.

Translated
by Paul
Selver

*N*o *literary movement can expect to hold for long the claim to modernism: when it writes the term on its banners, as in the case of the Modern Revue, the claim becomes an affront to a new generation. The illusionist baroque was in any case a delicate flower without deep roots. Even in their youth the Decadents had espoused the world-weary style of older men; and when in the new century fresh modernists called their eccentric ways passé, Decadence passed in graceful resignation to the world of decaying monuments which was part of their style. But the new generation owed much to the old. From them they both took a respect for formal artistry, and an attitude of social protest. But protest in their hands ceased to be abstract, ironical, nihilist, and became more positive and violent: the literary scene now reflected the social scene. During the years 1900 to 1914 hardly a year passed without serious rioting in the streets, nor could tough repressive measures stop student demonstrations from repeatedly getting out of hand. New literary work showed a sense of urgency towards contemporary problems, and a desire to bring art closer to contemporary life. The view of the writer as an isolated individualist gave way to one of him as an intellectual worker in a collective cause. Prague received from abroad the impulse of new styles—Cubism and functional art; Italian Futurism, Expressionism, and the modernism of Apollinaire. The young writers demanded above all that the voice of youth should be heard; proclaiming the world as their rightful heritage, they made life their cry, and coined the term Vitalism for their movement. Their work included poems of enthusiasm for the new world of technical civilization, but also naturalistic verse exalting the life of the instincts.*

Among the writers who successfully developed the Vitalist style was a poet who in fact belonged to an older generation: it was STANISLAV KOSTKA NEUMANN (1875-1947).

POLEDNE V SEČI

Stanislav
Kostka
Neumann
(1875-1947)

Mám plná ústa pryskyřic
a myslím, že utonu dnes
v zeleně proudech dychtivých,
jež se všech stran se řítí.
Je poledne. Ležím u seče.
Do vlažné trávy jsem kles'.
Po tichých deštích májových
vzduch hoří, chvěje se, svítí.

A já tu ležím pokořen
života bláznivým dnem,
jenž tryská, šílí, zpívá, žhne,
var pudů, hladů, žízní;
jsem zmámen vzruchem instinktů
a tvarů prchavým snem,
jež od země tihnou za sluncem
a syntheticky vyzní.

Mám plná ústa pryskyřic
a barev plničký zrak;
šum promíšených pohybů
jak moře v sluch mi hučí:
já ležím na dně, trosečník,
jenž opustil svůj vrak
a život pod hladinou ted'
se milovati učí.

360

MOON IN THE MOWING FIELDS

The spicy resins fill my mouth,
I feel that I shall drown
Beneath the greenly ardent tides
Rolled over me like rivers.
Noon in the mowing fields, and here
In warm grass I lie down.
After the soft May rains, the air
Scintillates, sparkles, quivers.

Round me, as I lie overwhelmed,
Life's sweet, mad heyday teems,
Delirious with heat and sound,
Hunger and joy and yearning;
Instincts and feelings daze my sense,
And shapes conceived in dreams,
Which steam from earth to seek the sun,
And fade beyond returning.

The spicy resins fill my mouth,
The colours fill my eyes,
My ears are loud with murmuring seas,
A ceaseless hum of motion.
I am a shipwrecked mariner
Who from his lost barque flies,
And changed, enchanted, learns to love
The deep-sea life of ocean.

Translated
by E.
Pargeter

*F*RÁŇA ŠRÁMEK *(1877-1952) seems in retrospect the most typical, and perhaps the most successful, poet of the Vitalist and Naturalist style. In his youth he wrote symbolist and Decadent poems: later he combined his literary role with a very active participation in political affairs. His support for the anarchist movement, and above all his fierce anti-militarist activity landed him more than once in gaol. Šrámek was conscripted during the First World War, and sent to the front: the traumatic experiences of this period are reflected in his verse, and he became one of the few successful Czech war poets. It is natural that a time of danger should draw men's attention to things which before went unnoticed and unappreciated: under stress, commonplace objects and experiences may become unbelievably precious, because our hold on them is so precarious: suddenly men cannot bear to part with things which before had been taken for granted. Thus the experience of war, with its emphasis on death, enlarged the consciousness of life, and what had been an aesthetic theme for the Vitalists, now acquired new reality. Šrámek's verse is at times almost childishly idyllic, at times primitive in its appeal to the senses—drunk with the promise of youth and nature, simple and touching, in revolt against intellectualism and aesthetic pose, yet with a note of melancholy which recalls old romanticism. Šrámek's best book of verse is The Weir—a book which still answers to many young people's ideas of what poetry ought to be like. Sentimentality is not too far away from Šrámek's verse, and it is not for every age or mood. Among his later novels was one, Moon over the River, a charming and nostalgic retrospect of the now aging poet. In the early 1950's, in the depths of Stalinist darkness in Prague the novel was filmed. In those strange circumstances the film had an extraordinary impact upon the Czech public, re-creating in its new setting a miracle of lost harmony—the greatest, and most unexpected, tribute to Šrámek's poetic gifts.*

SPLAV

Fráňa
Šrámek
(1877-1952)

Trápím se, trápím, myslím si,
kde bych tě nejraděj potkal.

Ulice střídám, parky a nábřeží,
bojím se krásných lží.
Bojím se lesa. V poledním lese
kdo miluje, srdce své neunese.
Na můj práh kdyby jsi vstoupila,
snad bys mne tím zabila.
Chtěl bych tě potkati v lukách.

V lukách je vlání
na všechny strany, pokorné odevzdávání.
V lukách je nejprostší života stůl,
rozlomíš chleba, podáš ženě půl,
chléb voní zemí, bezpečný úsměv svítí,
až k pláči je prostý věneček z lučního kvítí,
a oblaka jdou, přeběhlo světlo, přeběhl stín,
muž má touhu rozsévače,
žena má úrodný klín . . .

Chtěl bych tě potkati v lukách. Šel bych ti vstříc.
A až bys mi odešla, ach, z večera již,
bys na mne nemyslila víc,
jen na prosebný a děkovný můj hlas,
jako bych jen splavem byl,
který v lukách krásně zpívat slyšelas . . .

364

THE WEIR

Translated
by E.
Pargeter

I am vexed and fretted, thinking where
I should like best to meet with you.

I think in turn of parks, embankments, streets,
But fear their fair deceits.
I fear the woods, for in the noonday there
Love would be more than heart or soul could bear.
If you should cross my threshold, there would fill me
Such joy as well might kill me.
No, I would meet you in the meadows.

In meadows waves a grassy tide,
Humble, content, resigned, on every side.
The simplest sacrament of life is there,
Man and wife breaking bread in equal share,
Earth-scented bread, blessed by safe smiles and kind.
Touchingly simple is a wreath of meadow flowers entwined.
Clouds drive overhead, light passes, flying shadows loom,
Man has the sower's yearning,
Woman a fruitful womb—

In the meadows I would walk towards you, there should our
meeting be.
And when you went from me, ah, that very evening,
You'd think no more of me
But as a pleading, grateful voice still ringing
Distant and constant as the weir
That in the meadows you heard sweetly singing.

365

The life of KAREL TOMAN (1877-1946), who published his
first verses in the XIXth century, spans a sequence of literary development as varied as his own restless, troubled, and rebellious
life. He was a poet of personal lyric and social protest; of vigorous
self-assertion and melancholy resignation; an alienated and disin-
herited wanderer from his native land who returned, in the maturity of age, to the themes, scenes, and the cultural traditions of
his home. In his youth Karel Toman was among the artists whose
cry was Life, and whose spiritual home was not Prague, but Mont-
martre. The two poems printed below are from the years of
Toman's return; when his own summer was over, and the perils of
his native land drew him closer to its spirit. In the nature of this
sophisticated artist, the folk song lives again; and the appeal to
holy Wenceslas is a reminder of that cultural continuity which
runs like a golden thread through Czech literature.

367

V KLOBUKÁCH NA DUŠIČKY

Karel
Toman
(1877-1946)

Tuřanských zvonů tuším hlas,
kvílických lkání zaléhá sem.
Pokleknuv, hroby, mezi vás,
rozkolník osamělý dál jsem.

Hřbitove, duši víru dej
a požehnání domoviny
v ten zrádný čas, v zlý vlasti děj,
a odpusťte mi moje viny.

Nebudu výt s tím panstvem. Chci v tvou hlínu,
ať s prachem předků, s českou zemí splynu.

CEMETERY

I think I hear the bells of Turany,
their melancholy voices blow this way.
I kneel among your tombs;
I, a heretic and solitary.

Pour faith into my soul, cemetery,
and give my country your blessing;
my country, filthy in this time of treason;
and forgive me my trespasses.

I shall not slaver upon the new masters;
I shall hide in your heavy earth.
I shall mingle with my ancestors;
I shall mingle with Czech earth.

Translated
by Joy
Davidman

ZÁŘÍ

Karel
Toman

Můj bratr dooral a vypřáh koně.
A jak se stmívá,
věrnému druhu hlavu do hřívy
položil tiše, pohladil mu šíji
a zaposlouchal se, co mluví kraj.

Zní zvony z dálky tichým svatvečerem;
modlitba vesnic stoupá chladným šerem.
Duch země zpívá: úzkost, víra, bolest
v jediný chorál slily se a letí
k věčnému nebi.

Svatý Václave,
nedej zahynouti
nám ni budoucím.

370

SEPTEMBER

My brother has finished his ploughing, unharnessed the horses;
and now, in the gathering darkness
has quietly laid his head on the mane of his comrade
smoothing the neck; and begins to listen
to the voice of the country around him.

Far away sound the bells for the peaceful Eve of the Festival.
Through chill evening air arises the prayer of the villagers,
and the soul of the earth is in song: all anguish and faith and
   sorrow
are blended in one great hymn, and are soaring
up to the eternal skies.

Wenceslas, Holy one,
do not leave it to die into silence
for ourselves, or for men hereafter.

Translated by O. Elton